THERAPEUTIC APPROACH TO YOGA

SUDHESH CHAND S

Printed in India

ISBN:978-93-6045-744-0

First Printing, 2024

The Write Order

A division of Nasadiya Technologies Private Ltd.

Koramangala, Bangalore

Karnataka-560029

THE WRITE ORDER PUBLICATIONS.

www.thewriteorder.com

Edited by Ridham Bassi

Typeset by Aishwarya Wanjari

Book Cover designed by Keerthipriya PH

Publishing Consultant- Deeksha R

ABCS ON THERAPY YOGA FOR EVERYONE

A TEXTBOOK ON A PRACTICAL APPROACH TO THERAPY YOGA

What one can expect: This book offers comprehensive guidance for addressing the most common 7 ailments. It covers the pathophysiology and treatment measures from both an Ayurvedic and Allopathic perspective, provides yoga modifications, nutritional information, case studies, and much more.

TABLE OF CONTENTS

PREFACE

Yoga, once primarily practiced in India, is now embraced worldwide as a physical and mental fitness regimen. While various teachers are credited with spreading the knowledge of yoga, the practice has gained considerable momentum in recent years, thanks to the efforts of Prime Minister Narendra Modi, a staunch advocate and practitioner of yoga and Ayurveda. His endeavors have transformed the perception of yoga worldwide and increased its adoption as a means of wellness.

Yoga is an inclusive practice that people of all ages, genders, religions, and nationalities can enjoy. It is not limited to those who are physically fit but can also be beneficial for individuals who may be grappling with physical or mental health issues. Given the fast-paced and stress-inducing nature of modern life, it is crucial to care for our physical and mental well-being. Yoga offers a path to balance the energies within the body, a concept termed "alignment" by Guruji B.K.S. Iyengar. Yoga can also be a means to address health issues early on, which can have a positive impact on overall well-being.

During my early years, when I suffered from hyperacidity, I found that practicing yoga not only helped me overcome my condition but also gave me a deeper understanding of my body and mind, leading to a transformative change in my life. This inspired me to become a teacher and help people through the practice of yoga.

In the last four decades of my practice and teaching, I have encountered various practitioners who primarily focus on the physical aspect of yoga (asanas). While it is a good place to start, in today's fast-paced and stress-prone world, addressing the physical aspects alone will not guarantee overall benefits in the long run. The practice of yoga becomes subtle and comprehensive when the mind, body, and breath are in harmony. As one learns to synchronize movement with breath, the experience becomes nuanced. To achieve this, practice, patience, and perseverance are a must. This may be challenging at first, but as the practice becomes a discipline over time, the mind opens to different dimensions of this ancient technique and brings about transformative changes in the practitioner: mentally, physically, and emotionally.

During my early years as a teacher, I encountered practitioners who were healthy as well as those with health conditions, both mental and physical. As people started seeing the benefits of yoga as a discipline by practicing regularly, their positive feedback spread through word of mouth, and many started approaching me for therapeutic yoga for their health issues, such as hypertension, asthma, back pain, and neck pain. The prospect of helping people manage their health conditions through the practice of yoga fascinated me, and I started diving deeper into this field. I was fortunate enough to learn from esteemed teachers such as Shri Karunakarji, Shri Muraliji, and Shri Raghavendra Shenoyji. I also learned from the videos of Shri B.K.S. Iyengar Ji. This is how I got into the art of therapeutic yoga.

For the past 15 years, I have been practicing yoga therapy and have come across people with conditions such as transverse myelitis, Parkinson's disease, ataxia, thyroid imbalance, cerebral palsy, bell's palsy, diabetes, nasal allergies, lumbar issues, cervical issues, acidity, knee pain, digestive disorders, frozen shoulders, obesity, infertility, hyperkyphosis, PCOD, and asthma.

One of the key benefits of being a therapist is gaining a deeper understanding of the nature of various health conditions. Over time, I have developed a passion for studying specific health conditions and have learned to create personalized practices for individuals based on their level of mobility. Understanding the complexities of these health conditions and developing programs tailored to the individual's abilities has been a significant accomplishment and a fulfilling experience for me.

I encourage all yoga teachers to develop an interest in therapeutic yoga. This will help them understand their own bodies better, and once they learn about the therapeutic benefits of yoga, they can, in turn, help others manage or overcome their health challenges.

In this book, I have explained how yoga therapy can be used to manage or overcome 10 distinct ailments. The content in this book is based on my experience with the many cases I have encountered throughout my teaching experience so far. I am grateful to my students for their willingness to share their stories so that we could delve deeply into the therapeutic benefits of yoga. I am also thankful to the medical community, other teachers, and other sources such as books, videos, and research papers that have helped us validate and expand our understanding.

Globally, there is an increasing awareness of alternative therapies, and yoga therapy is becoming one of the most prominent and widely accepted forms of such therapies. I believe that this book will provide hope and solutions for those seeking to manage imbalances in the body through yoga therapy, especially if they are frustrated with poor results after long periods of medical treatment and surgical interventions.

"MAY THE BLESSINGS OF YOGA SHOWER LIGHT ON ALL OF US."

ABOUT US

SUDHESH CHAND S

Sudhesh Chand is an experienced yoga teacher with over 35 years of teaching experience and the founder of Shri Upanishath Yoga Center Trust in Mysore. He has taught thousands of students across the globe. His yoga journey began over 41 years ago when he focused on improving his health. Along the way, he mastered yoga and started to help hundreds of people recover their physical and mental health by guiding them in the true practice of yoga.

He learned from respected yoga teachers and gurus such as Mohan Bhargav, Shri Shri Nagaraja, Surya Narayana Pandeyji, Shri Raghavendra Shenoy, Rope Murali, Karunakar Puttur, and others. He has been imparting the knowledge of traditional yoga not only in India but in many countries across Europe, the United Kingdom, China, United States Of America. He conducted yoga workshops for the faculty and students at IIT Ropar, Punjab (2016–2018). He also worked at Wai Lana's Yoga Center in Sanya (South China) as a teacher's trainer for a short period.

He has been actively involved in various activities in the field of yoga, including conducting demonstrations, teaching, training, and guiding practitioners. He has played key roles in various institutions and organizations in the preparation of presentations and the processing of large-scale information on yoga. He has conducted workshops, counseling sessions, guest lectures, and public talks in the area of stress management. He has striven hard to establish yoga as a means for physical and mental health. He takes an active interest in social causes as well.

He has written and published two books in Kannada related to yoga, namely "Jeevanada Jyothi Yoga" in 2006 and "Yoga Aarogya Jyothi" in 2011, whose second edition was recently published in 2022. He conducts a regular Hatha Yoga Teachers Training Course (HYT 200) as well as a therapy teachers training course. He has conducted a certification course for more than 30 physical education directors at Mysore University and has also released around 14 DVDs featuring topics related to yoga.

He provides yoga therapy sessions for different ailments like back pain, slip disc, herniated disc, sciatica, ataxia, cerebral palsy, bell's palsy, arrhythmia, transverse myelitis, nasal allergies, thyroid imbalance, Parkinson's disease, and many more.

He has been honored by various universities and institutions for his work in yoga.

To name a few:

- Yogaottama Shree" award from K N Foundation, Bengaluru on 8th October 2023.

- “Champaka Kalarathna” award from Champaka Education And Cultural Trust Regd, Mysuru on 1st June 2023.
- "Yoga Visharada" award from Mysore Vivekananda Yoga Education & Research Center on June 19, 2016.
- "Yogasana Praveena" award from Swaralaya Sangeetha Samsthe in the year 2015.

Some other instances of honor and appreciation rendered to him were the following:

- Oscar Fernandes, Central Minister, 2009.
- "Indira Gandhi National Center for the Arts," New Delhi, on March 29, 2009.
- The Chartered Accountant Association.
- ING Vysya.
- "Indian Society of Anaesthesiologists Isacon 2006" at Lalitha Mahal Palace.
- Mahila Samakhya, Women's Organization at JSS Law College.
- Wipro at its premises in Mysore.

RAJEEV ANANTHARAMAN IYER

Rajeev, an engineering professional, was hard at work in the tech industry for over a decade when he was diagnosed with a lumbar disc issue. The doctors informed him that this condition was mainly caused by the wrong posture he adopted during long hours of sitting and working in his office. This diagnosis occurred in 2015, and Rajeev embarked on his journey to full recovery by doing back-strengthening exercises taught to him by the doctor.

He didn't stop with just practicing these stretches but began to dedicate his recovery period to learning and understanding more about the causes, effects, and other issues related to his problem. He also conducted his own research on how to alleviate his back pain. Although initially, his focus was solely on getting rid of the back pain, he decided to develop a routine for physical activity and joined a fitness center in Bangalore.

Here, he explored various forms of workouts, including strengthening and conditioning, high-intensity interval training, boxing, and CrossFit. It was during this time that he was introduced to yoga. He noticed that many of the stretches recommended by the doctor were related to some asanas in yoga. Over time, the practice of yoga significantly helped him correct his posture, and the back pain disappeared. He realized that it was only through yoga that he could develop a mind-body-breath connection and bring about a transformation in himself. So, he decided to pursue his passion for yoga.

In 2020, he made the decision to leave the tech industry and enroll in a teacher training program. His search for a guru continued until he found Shri Upanishath Yoga Center Trust in Kuvempu Nagar, Mysore, where he completed his 200-hour teacher training under the guidance of Guru Sri Sudhesh Chand. The teacher training program provided him with a deeper understanding of the inner self and how yoga can help bring about a lifestyle change by improving overall health.

By this point, he was fully convinced of the remarkable power of yoga to heal the body and was fascinated by the many things he had discovered about the therapeutic aspects of yoga. This led him to complete his yoga therapy teacher's training. This program enabled him to understand the subtler aspects of yoga, which included modifications and variations based on an individual's range of movement, considering the student's health condition, and the use of props. He is now an active practitioner and is training students from around the world through his online and offline classes.

SHALINI AITHAL

Shalini is a trained psychologist with a passion for yoga and helping others. She has devoted her life to combining her expertise in mental health with the healing power of yoga to assist individuals in achieving optimal well-being.

She completed extensive training in teaching yoga at the Sri Upanishath Yoga Centre in Kuvempu Nagar, Mysore, under the guidance of yoga guru Sri Sudhesh Chand.

Her personal experience with sciatica pain had a significant impact on her passion for therapy and yoga. During her time as a transcriptionist, she endured intense pain in her lower back and legs due to long hours of sitting in one place. This pain had a detrimental effect on her physical health, making her acutely aware of the importance of maintaining a healthy body. This experience of intense pain prevented her from performing regular asanas, and she was introduced to therapy yoga. She found great relief from this pain, which further fueled her passion for therapy and yoga.

Following this experience, she undertook and completed extensive training in teaching yoga and therapy yoga at the Sri Upanishath Yoga Centre in Kuvempunagar, Mysore, under the guidance of yoga guru Sri Sudhesh Chand. This training equips her to help others experience relief from various physical and mental health concerns.

While working on assignments for the course and assisting for this book, which spanned about 28 months, she gained a deeper understanding of yoga as a form of therapy for various physical conditions. She realized the healing power of yoga and thoroughly enjoyed the journey while observing therapy yoga in action and its positive impact on individuals with different ailments at the Sri Upanishath Yoga Centre in Kuvempu Nagar, Mysore.

She has worked with numerous clients suffering from various ailments and has successfully helped them find relief through therapy and yoga under the guidance of her guru, Sri Sudhesh Chand. She is profoundly grateful for the opportunity to be a part of the journey in assisting for the book and to witness the positive impact that therapy and yoga can have on individuals struggling with physical health issues.

R. P. AMRUTHA PRAVEEN

Amrutha graduated in Commerce with Computer Science and is a businessperson with a passion for yoga, meditation, and being part of the transformative journey of people through the aforementioned practices. She hails from the city of Proddatur. Her parents instilled in her an interest in yoga by introducing her to the practice when she was ten years old. They also educated her about how yoga kept her active and healthy. She began by practicing yoga during the weekends and later became a regular practitioner.

After her marriage, she moved to Mysore and enrolled in yoga classes with Guru Sudhesh Chand at the Upanishath Yoga Center. Her guru had the practice of giving individual attention to students and took the time not only to teach but also to explain how regular yoga practice can bring about positive changes in life. This deepened her interest in the practice of yoga.

Having practiced meditation as well and taught it to many people, she felt that the combined effect of regular yoga and meditation had brought about many positive changes in her own physical and mental health. She became curious about the science of yoga and how it affects the body. Yoga also had a positive effect on the mind and thoughts. She believed that the study of yoga could help numerous people suffering from poor health, especially due to hormonal imbalances.

She completed the Therapy Teacher's Training Program and found answers to many of the questions she had had for several years. Her training has helped her become better at teaching meditation and counseling those who reach out to her for help.

Photography credit goes to Ajay Vittal: @ajayvittalphotography

I am Ajay Vittal, a software engineer working for a private company in Mysuru. As I developed an interest and passion for birds, I took up bird photography a few years ago. Upon the request of my Yoga guru, Shri. Sudhesh Chand, I have captured most of the yoga photographs featured in this book. I am grateful to him for giving me the opportunity to be associated with his dream project.

The joint and muscle action sections are reviewed and amended by Dr. Bhanu Krupa:

Dr. Banu Krupa P.T., Chief Physiotherapist at PRAISHA Physiotherapy Center, Mysore Certified Dry Needling Practitioner Certified IASTM Practitioner London Shoulder Clinic: Certified Practitioner

Ayurveda sections are reviewed and amended by Beatrice Deschamps:

Beatrice Deschamps holds an MD in corporate finance and a BAMS degree from Gujarat Ayurveda University, DU Pharmacy, Lille, France. She is a certified yoga instructor with 200 hours of training at Kaivalyadhama, Pune. Beatrice has undergone numerous intensive training programs in Kaya Chikitsa and Sanskrit in India in 2019, 2020, 2022, and 2023. She is the founder of "Heart of Ayurveda," dedicated to raising awareness and promoting Ayurveda in France. Additionally, she authors a blog on Ayurveda in French and co-authored the book "Ayurveda Family Guidebook" in French in 2022.

Nutrition sections are reviewed and amended by Shradda Krishna:

Shradda Krishna is a certified yoga teacher and nutritionist. She completed her Hatha Yoga TTC under the guidance of Mr. Sudhesh Chand in Mysore. Shradda has a background in research-based nutrition, having undertaken general nutrition and clinical nutrition courses from the NFNA (National Fitness and Nutrition Academy) in Kolkata.

AUTHOR'S ACKNOWLEDGEMENTS

I express gratitude to Rajeev Anantharaman Iyer, Amrutha Praveen, Shalini Aithal, Rani Tryambeke, Preethi Verma, and Lavanya Purushottam for their invaluable contributions to our discussions, manuscript drafting, and participation in the asana photo shoot featured in this book.

I extend my sincere gratitude to Dr. Bhanu Krupa for her patience and time dedicated to guiding us in the joint and main muscle actions section. Additionally, I am indebted to Dr. Beatrice Deschamps for generously offering her time to guide us in the Ayurveda section, and to Shradda Krishna for her valuable insights and guidance in the nutrition section of this book.

I am profoundly grateful to Ajay Vittal, whose invaluable contribution of time and skill in capturing the photos of the asanas for this book using his camera is truly appreciated. Words cannot adequately express my thanks for his dedication and expertise.

I wish to convey my deepest gratitude to Dr. Goutham Cugati, Dr. Deepak, Dr. Vijay, Dr. Praveen, Dr. Hema Shivalingaiah, Dr. Lalitha Ravi, and Dr. Sudha Rao for generously dedicating their precious time to read the contents and validate their views. Their insightful contributions add significant weight to this book, and I am truly thankful for their expertise and support.

The realization of this endeavor would not have been possible without the unwavering support and trust exhibited by the students of our Yoga Centre. Their steadfast commitment has played a pivotal role in the success of this project.

Undertaking this journey would have been impossible without the immense overall support of my wife, Nandini, and son, Abhishreshta. Their unwavering encouragement and understanding have been indispensable throughout this endeavor.

I extend special thanks to Supreetha Suresh, Nagalakshmi Pumagame, and Amrutha Praveen for their generous and monetary support. Their kindness has been instrumental in the success of this endeavor, and I am truly grateful for their contributions.

My heartfelt thanks extend to Write Order Publications and every team member involved in transforming this remarkable project into a book format. Their commitment to the responsibilities of formatting, advertising, marketing, printing, and publishing has played a crucial role in presenting this work to the world, and I am sincerely grateful for their efforts.

Last but not least, I would like to express my sincere pranaams to Dr. N. V. Krishnamurthy for his patience in reading the entire book and providing his insightful views in the foreword, which holds significant importance for this publication. His contribution has added a valuable dimension to the book, and I am truly grateful for his time and expertise.

FOREWORD

The global desire for health, happiness, prosperity, and peace is universal, yet the pursuit of a life filled with abundance, joy, good health, and internal peace is a question worth pondering. Ancient practices like Ayurveda and Yoga offer proven holistic approaches to balance and harmonize body, mind, and spiritual health. In today's fast-paced world, physical and mental ailments often stem from ignorance and misplaced priorities, but these can be addressed or prevented through time-tested methods.

Yoga, incorporating physical postures, breathing techniques, and meditation, is a systematic practice promoting wellness and higher consciousness. Despite its growing popularity in the West, a significant number of Indians still perceive it as esoteric, seeking quick fixes elsewhere for chronic issues. Wider dissemination of knowledge and events like 'Yoga Day' could enhance awareness of traditional medical and therapeutic systems.

The term "Yoga" derives from the Sanskrit root 'yuj,' signifying union, aligning the microcosm (individual) with the macrocosm (universe). Yoga's impact extends beyond physical and mental health, addressing the interplay of fundamental elements (earth, fire, water, air, and ether) inside and outside the body to manage mental stress, a leading cause of ailments.

Yoga's benefits span all ages and health conditions, becoming an integral part of treatment plans. Scientific studies highlight its efficacy in areas like arthritis, oncology, chronic pain, and more. Stress, a major contributor to illness, can be effectively managed through yoga, offering composure and improved well-being.

Human challenges, rooted in ego, ignorance, and arrogance, can lead to downfall. The choice lies in whether individuals strive for their immense potential, attaining higher consciousness through yoga, or lead ordinary lives in ignorance. Awareness of one's koshas, doshas, and chakras becomes crucial, with the power of ancient Indian wisdom evident in practices like pranayama, which can delay the inevitable visit of Yama (Yamaraja) for as long as possible, preserving life force (prana).

I am privileged to discuss the remarkable book "Therapeutic Approach to Yoga" by Sri Sudhesh Chand. Having known him for years as a dedicated yoga teacher, he has played a crucial role in healing numerous patients through proven yoga therapies. The 'Shri Upanishath Yoga Centre Trust,' founded by him in Mysore, is globally recognized for its significant service to the needy. Sri Sudhesh Chand's extensive research in this field is evident in his multiple authored books, serving as valuable guides for many Hatha Yoga teachers.

Among the myriad books on Yoga and related subjects, this particular one distinguishes itself through its excellence, simplicity, and ease of understanding. The book's unique quality lies in its yogic approach to address seven common ailments, presented in straightforward language. It covers diagnosis, easy-to-follow yoga postures (including do's and don'ts), nutritional aspects, and incorporates contextual references to both Ayurveda and allopathy for comprehensive understanding.

The author's commendable approach is evident as leading allopathic specialists in domains such as lumbar and spinal treatment, diabetes mellitus, thyroid issues, arthritis, gastroenterology, vascular diseases, and stress management have thoroughly vetted and validated the contents of this book. This consultative process reflects the author's care and sincerity in ensuring that the sensitive topic of health management is disseminated after thorough research and backed by the robust knowledge resources of modern medicine. By combining insights from both ancient and modern systems, this book emerges as a well-validated, comprehensive resource for doctors, yoga teachers, therapists, nutritionists, and, most importantly, ailing patients seeking relief from chronic ailments.

Another compelling aspect of the book is the inclusion of personal experiences from the practitioner's perspective. Sri R. A Iyer shares insights into the transformative power of yoga, while Smt. Shalini Aithal recounts her discovery of the benefits of yoga in healing psychological ailments. Additionally, Smt. Amrutha Praveen's success in meditation and counseling adds a valuable dimension to the book, providing real-life examples of how individuals have benefited from these practices. This personal touch enhances the book's relatability and underscores the practical impact of yoga on individuals' well-being.

I extend my congratulations to the author, Sri Sudhesh Chand, for producing this excellent book. I am confident that it will be warmly received and appreciated, serving as a valuable benchmark on the highly sought-after subject of health and well-being.

I extend my best wishes to everyone involved in the creation of this wonderful book. May you all find success and fulfillment in your pursuits.

Om Shanthi.

Dr. N. V. Krishnamurthy,

Director and Chief Consultant Physician,

PRAJNA KUTEERA,

100/2, Vishwamanava Double Road,

Kergalli, Jayapura Hobli,

Mysore, 570026

12th January 2024

REVIEW FROM THE DOCTORS

Review from Dr. Goutham Cugati for Lumbar Issues:

This is a unique work where each of the topics has been discussed under allopathy and the appropriate explanation of intervention in yoga. The detailed manner in which the yoga postures and the alternatives have been provided, along with demonstrations, makes this book a masterpiece.

I recommend this book, which has every detail of the discussed topic with reasoning, to all yoga enthusiasts to improve their knowledge.

Dr. Goutham Cugati

Consultant Neurosurgeon

Mysore

Review from Dr. Deepak for Diabetes:

The contents are clear, up to the point, and in accordance with the recent diabetes guidelines. The treatment mentioned is evidence-based and in accordance with current guidelines for diabetic patients. The nutritional aspect of diabetic management is well-elaborated and apt. The importance of low-GI foods and carbs as the last approach is well highlighted.

The basic pathological mechanism of type 2 diabetes, which is the most common type of diabetes, is insulin resistance. Exercise reduces insulin resistance and, hence, helps greatly with sugar control. The exercises and asanas mentioned are helpful in decreasing the insulin resistance in the skeletal muscles and, hence, improving glucose and lowering blood glucose. In the current era of the diabetic pandemic, this chapter clearly highlights the pathophysiology of diabetes mellitus, insulin resistance, and lifestyle modification. It highlights the importance of yoga and exercises that would help reduce insulin resistance. The breathing pattern and pranayama would reduce stress and control hormone secretion. I personally found the explanations in simple, understandable language, and hence they are very appealing.

The photographs are clear and depict the proper method of performing a particular asana.

Dr. Deepak General Medicine

General Medicine

Mysore

Review on Gastritis by Dr. Lalitha Ravi:

This book is extensively researched and very well written. 'Do not exercise immediately after food' is a phrase popularized by science now, but our yoga gurus have said this for thousands of years.

This book is all about yoga and lifestyle modifications, which are much needed for the present life routine with stress and unhealthy eating habits. There are added benefits to dos and don'ts in the nutrition segment, which could help in managing gastritis in the long run. It is possible that these postures with modifications would make it easier for everyone to do asanas and benefit in treating gastritis, which is notoriously difficult to manage with allopathy.

It was a pleasure reading this book.

Dr. Lalitha Ravi

Senior Family Physician

Mysore

Review on Arthritis by Dr. Vijay:

The contents of the book are good and informative, even for common people. The holistic approach with NSAIDs, knee-strengthening exercises, and hydrotherapy will be helpful for people suffering from arthritis. The treatment mentioned in the book is good, but when severe pain is not subsided, intra-articular steroid injections, etc. are recommended to manage the pain.

I definitely feel this book is very helpful, even for a layman. Warm-up exercises, regular walking, and modified asanas with props would help strengthen the muscles, bones, and joints.

The photos are very clear, making it easy to understand the postures. I would even recommend making YouTube videos and sharing the link with patients so that they can benefit more.

Overall, this is a good education and an overview of treatment on the topic of arthritis. I would like to add that, with all the above information, sun exposure and vitamin D synthesis knowledge would also benefit the majority of patients.

Dr. Vijay

Associate Professor, Department of Orthopaedics

J. S. S. Hospital

Mysore

Review of Stress by Dr. Hema Shivalingaiah:

The topic is very well explained. Readers will understand each asana. The topic explained is clear, useful, and easy to understand even for laymen. I have shared some of the points which are also included. The photographs are clear enough to understand.

Dr. Hema Shivalingaiah

Associate Professor of Cardiology

Sri Jayadeva Institute of Cardiovascular Sciences

Mysuru

Review on Thyroid by Dr. Praveen N.S.:

The contents discussed are enough for public understanding. It is very informative for the layman. The treatment methods explained in allopathy are good. The photographs are clear enough and understandable.

Dr. Praveen

N.S. Assistant Professor Endocrinologist

K. R. Hospital

Mysuru

Review of Varicose Veins by Dr. Sudha Rao:

My hearty congratulations on a very well-written book. It contains about 7 chapters on diseases in which yoga therapy is very useful for treatment. I appreciate the presentation of each chapter, which starts with a brief description, cause, symptoms, and diagnosis, followed by yoga therapy. I particularly like the photographs, which will help a lot of people understand better. The authors deserve good encouragement.

Dr. Sudha Rao

M.B.B.S., M.D.G.O.

Retired Professor of Obstetrics and Gynecology

Mysore

MY APPROACH TOWARDS YOGA THERAPY

My journey into yoga began in 1981 when I was suffering from severe hyperacidity. Yoga was not so popular then, but one of my friends, Mr. Dayananda, suggested that I should find a yoga teacher to help me with my illness. Incidentally, my father, who was working in a hotel in Hyderabad, wrote a letter to me to buy a yoga book for his manager and send it to him.

It was like a blessing to me, and I purchased a yoga book from the Gowrishankara book depot adjacent to Devaraja Market in Mysore. I was curious to know about the contents of the book, and before sending it to my father, I read through it, where I came across some poses that were recommended as beneficial to those who experienced acidity. I mentally noted the steps to perform those poses and started practicing them. To my surprise, I could feel a lot of improvement in my health. I personally experienced the therapeutic power of yoga. It was remarkable to me because I was cured of a physical ailment without much medical intervention. And this is when I started buying books related to yoga, particularly those written by Guruji Shri B. K. S. Iyengar.

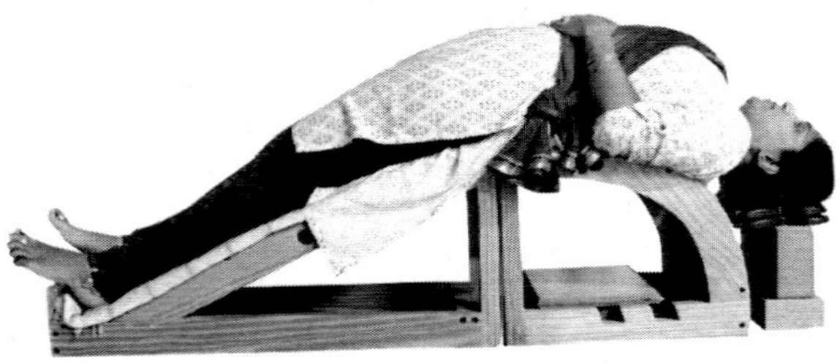

Many years later, in 1997, I began experiencing severe back pain and was unable to stand or walk, and upon consulting a doctor, my condition was diagnosed as sciatica. This was also a stumbling block for my practice since, when I attempted to practice, I experienced excessive pain. Although this went on for six months, this painful experience was also a turning point for me and my practice. As I wanted to continue practicing, I started modifying certain poses, which helped me with my pain.

I gained a new perspective on how standard practices could be personalized and customized to the needs of the practitioner. Within a few months, I recovered completely from Sciatica. This personal experience inspired me to modify many poses to suit practitioners who were suffering from a variety of ailments.

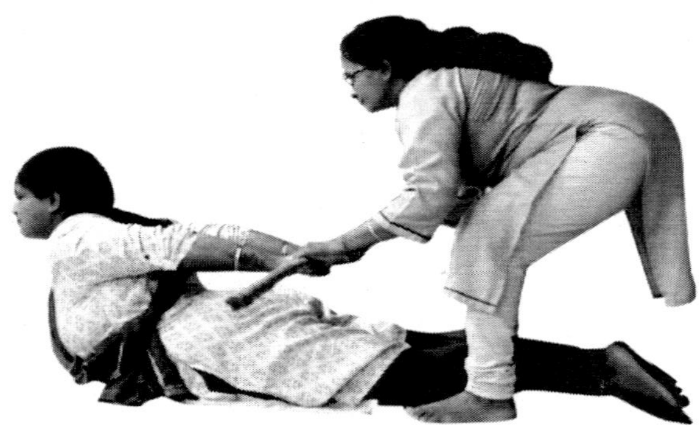

I had continued practicing by myself and was only giving private sessions at homes where people required them and at some centers such as Dhvanya Loka, Cosmopolitan Club, and Shri Raghavendra Yoga Center. I started my yoga center Shri Upanishath Yoga Centre in 2003 in Kuvempunagar, Mysore, India.

My teaching skills improved tremendously after I started my own center. When my students struggled to perform some of the steps exactly as mentioned in the books, I trained them to modify their poses. This motivated my students, and they started to practice with interest and attended the sessions continuously without dropping out or taking leave.

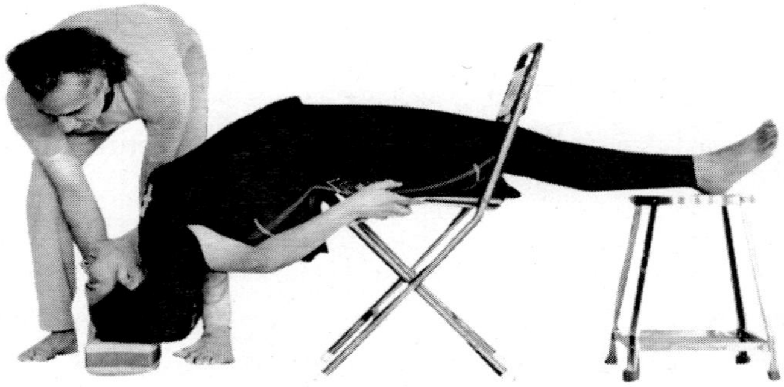

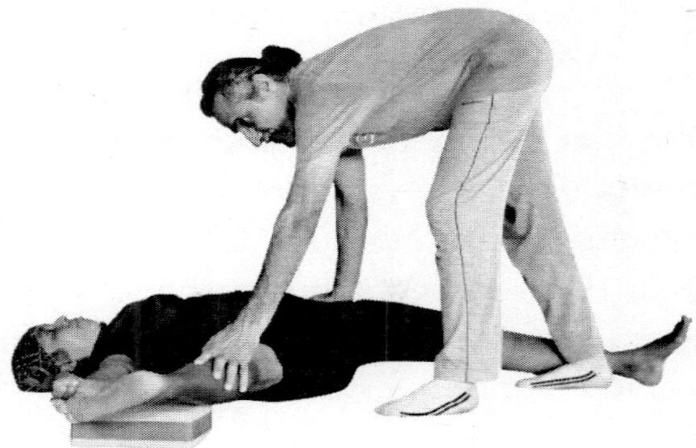

This concept of modifying the pose with the expertise of using props helped me in training students who came with various health issues, and the results they achieved were tremendous, which prompted me to start therapy yoga sessions in the year 2008. From there on, there was no looking back. My greatest success in the years that followed was helping people (practitioners) get relief from their health issues. These practitioners, in turn, started recommending therapeutic yoga to others. Even doctors started referring their patients for yoga therapy at our center.

My experience has convinced me that yoga therapy should be introduced in every yoga institute. I request that my fellow practitioners use it as an alternate therapy to improve people's health.

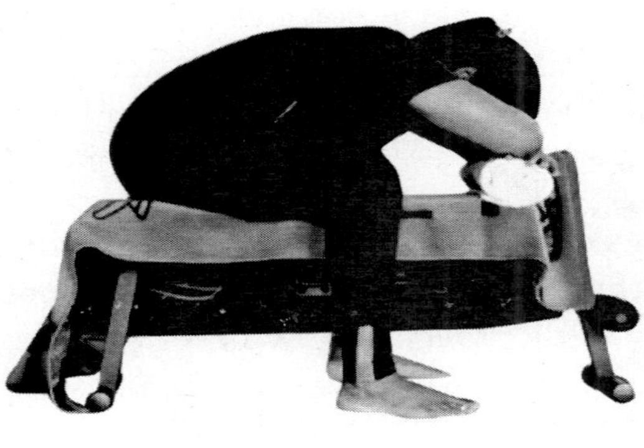

INSIGHT INTO THERAPY YOGA

Yoga, one of the oldest and most valuable disciplines rooted in ancient wisdom, is a gift from India to the modern world. It has been practiced for centuries by ancient sages, scholars, and intellectuals and taught to learners to promote health, happiness, and harmony. Yoga is now widely accepted as a form of healing and treatment, alongside traditional medical practices and surgical interventions. The practice of asanas (postures), pranayama (breathing techniques), and dhyana (meditation) can lead to significant improvements in health and longevity.

Yoga should not be viewed as a rigorous regime to be performed to achieve the best results. Instead, it should be approached as a gentle practice designed to promote overall health and well-being. Therefore, practitioners should be mindful to perform the breathing and postures correctly; otherwise, they may risk injury.

While traditional yoga practice can be highly beneficial, therapeutic yoga is a growing field that uses evidence-based research to address specific health conditions. As the world continues to evolve, many people continue to move to urban centers and start to lead sedentary lifestyles. Such individuals also eat late, sleep late, and work late, which can drain their energy and contribute to a range of health issues. Yoga therapy can help to reconnect the mind and body and can be easily incorporated into a daily routine to promote mindfulness and reduce stress.

Recently, a growing number of physicians are recognizing the benefits of yoga for overall health. While yoga is not a replacement for traditional medicine, it can be a complementary therapy for patients with chronic illnesses.

The practice of yoga includes asanas (postures), pranayama (breathing exercises), and dhyana (meditation) in one session. Research has shown that regular practice of these sessions can lead to significant improvements in regulating blood pressure and heart rate, reducing stress levels by decreasing or regulating the production of cortisol (a stress hormone), and increasing levels of serotonin, which stabilizes mood.

Furthermore, the therapeutic benefits of yoga are most effectively seen when a program is designed, taking the health condition and range of movement of the practitioner into consideration. Such a program would include poses with variations or modifications, breathing techniques, and the use of props to make the pose more comfortable to achieve. This makes yoga therapy a highly personalized session for individuals, setting it apart from a typical yoga session. Unlike regular yoga teachers, yoga therapists are highly skilled, trained, and experienced professionals who design and teach yoga with the help of props that are necessary for certain individuals.

Yoga is often initially viewed as a physical practice for fitness and weight loss, but it offers much more than that. To truly experience the benefits of yoga, one must coordinate their breathing with movement, which develops awareness. As awareness becomes the primary focus, the practice evolves, and the benefits of yoga become apparent.

While yoga therapy may have limitations, such as not being able to cure certain chronic diseases, it can still be beneficial in terms of managing the condition. For example, regular yoga practice can help a person prepare for surgery by making them more mentally relaxed and physically strong. Yoga therapy has also shown positive results in treating conditions such as stress, hypertension, back pain, neck pain, spinal issues, heart conditions, asthma, chronic fatigue, headaches, diabetes, Parkinson's disease, ataxia, allergies, and so on.

In yoga, props are used to support and enhance the practice of yoga asanas (poses). The use of props can help people achieve proper alignment, improve balance, and deepen their stretches.

Here is a list of props used during our work:

- **Blocks:** Blocks are made of foam, cork, or wood and are used to bring the floor closer to the practitioner. Blocks can be used for standing poses, seated poses, and even inversions.
- **Straps/Belt:** Straps are long pieces of fabric or leather that can be used to extend the reach of the arms or legs in seated and standing poses. They can also be used to deepen stretches and hold poses for longer periods.
- **Mini Mattress:** Blankets can be used for cushioning and support in seated poses and for padding under the knees or hips in kneeling poses. They can also be used to support the back in reclined poses.
- **Bolster:** Bolsters are cylindrical or rectangular cushions that can be used to support the back, hips, or legs in reclined poses. They can also provide cushioning and support in seated poses.
- **Chair:** Chairs can provide support and stability in standing poses, especially for practitioners with limited mobility or injuries. They can also be used for seated poses and practicing inversions.
- **Wall:** Walls can offer support in standing poses and help with practicing inversions. They can also aid in alignment and deepen stretches.
- **Wooden Stick:** A wooden stick, also known as a yoga stick or staff, is a prop used in yoga to assist with balance, alignment, and deeper stretches. The stick is typically made of wood, bamboo, or similar sturdy material and can vary in length depending on the practitioner's height and needs.
- **Wheel:** It is a circular, wheel-shaped prop made of foam, plastic, or wood and can vary in size and density.

- **Back Bender:** A back bender is a prop used in yoga to assist with back-bending poses. It is a curved prop made of foam, plastic, or wood designed to support the spine and open the chest in back-bending poses.
- **Gymnastic Ball:** A gymnastic ball, or yoga ball, is a prop used in yoga therapy to support a variety of poses and movements. It is a large, inflatable ball made of durable material and comes in various sizes depending on the practitioner's height and needs.
- **Mini Stool:** A mini stool, also known as a yoga stool, is a prop used in yoga therapy to support a variety of poses and movements. It is a small stool made of wood or metal and can be used to support the hands or feet in various poses and movements.
- **Rope & S-Hook:** Ropes and S-hooks are props used in Iyengar Yoga, a form of yoga therapy that focuses on precision and alignment. These props help practitioners deepen their practice by providing support and extension in various poses.
- **Sandbag:** Sandbags can be a useful prop in yoga therapy, providing a gentle but firm weight that helps the body release tension and relax more deeply into poses.

Using props can help practitioners achieve the full benefits of a yoga practice while minimizing the risk of injury. Props also enable practitioners to modify poses to suit their individual needs and abilities.

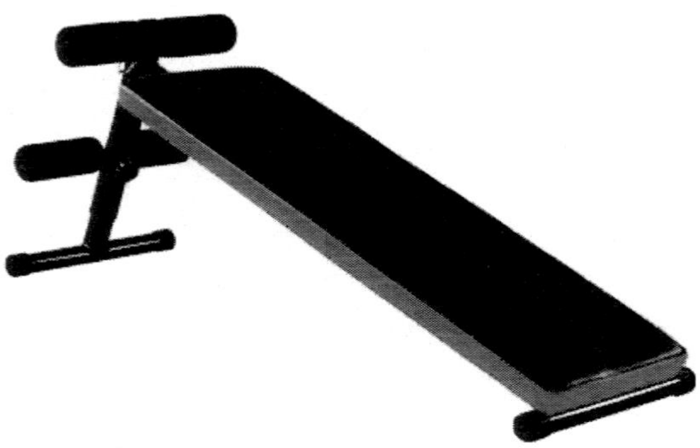
Abs bench

Back bender bench

Gymnastic Ball

Yoga Blocks

Mini mattress

Mini Stool

Sand Bag

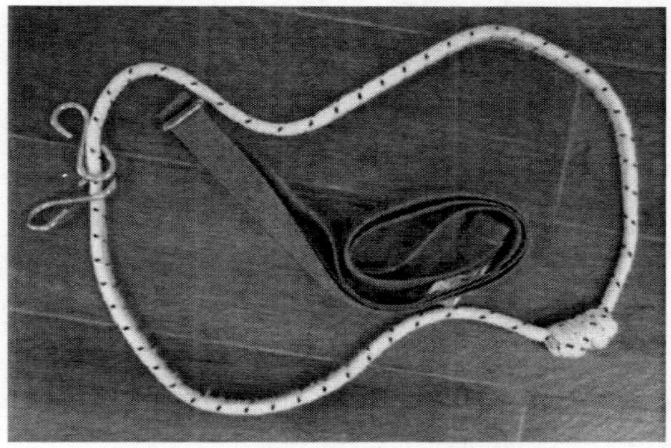

Rope, S-hook and Strap

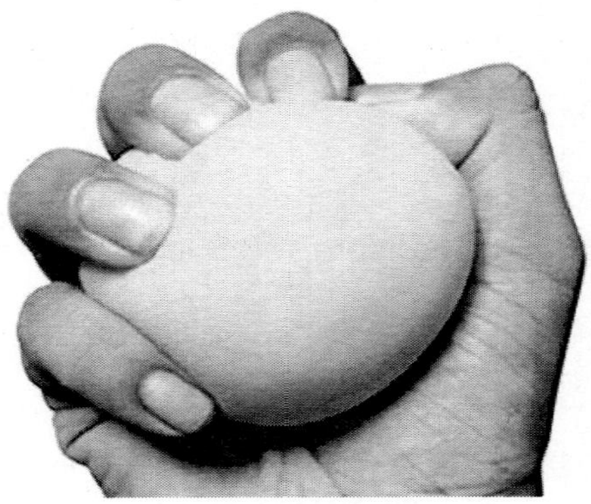

Soft Ball

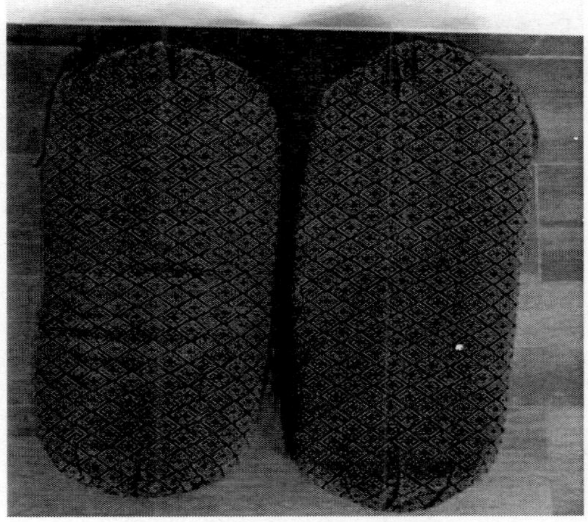

Thick Cotton bolsters

Yoga Chair

Yoga Wheel and Wooden Stick

Yoga therapy is gaining popularity and demand, and individuals can now choose it as a career to provide a holistic healing method for patients. Many doctors recommend it to their patients, and medical journals are publishing research on the numerous benefits of yoga therapy. One notable example of this positive trend is the work of Dr. Dean Ornish, a cardiologist from the United States who has developed a yoga-based therapy for heart disease that has proven to be so successful that it is covered by public health insurance. Even the NHS in the United Kingdom includes yoga therapy as part of its complementary and alternative therapy services.

Reference: https://themindedinstitute.com/

In the words of T. K. V Desikachar:

"Yoga therapy is a self-empowering process where the care seeker, with the help of a therapist, implements a personalized and evolving yoga practice. This practice not only addresses the illness in a multi-dimensional manner but also aims to alleviate suffering progressively, non-invasively, and as a complementary approach. Depending on the nature of the illness, yoga therapy can be preventive, curative, or serve as a means to manage the illness or facilitate healing at all levels."

YOGA FOR EVERYONE

Yoga is laudable for its ability to reduce emotional disturbances in the human mind and instill a sense of peace and power in the practitioner. However, it's important to note that one size does not fit everyone. With individual needs, abilities, and desires varying, the guru tailors the course to suit each student's unique requirements.

Before a student embarks on the practice of yoga, it is crucial for the guru to consider factors such as the student's specific needs, interests, health, age, and cultural background. Armed with this essential background information, the guru can then pinpoint the right approach that maximizes the benefits of yoga practice for that particular student. This underscores the importance of practicing yoga under the guidance of a guru. While individuals may have specific goals in mind, the expertise of a skilled teacher can help them grasp the deeper essence of yoga, extending beyond the physical aspects.

The teacher-student relationship plays a pivotal role in determining the appropriate practice for each individual. A skilled teacher can guide the students in understanding and practicing yoga in a way that caters to their specific needs and abilities. Practicing yoga under the guidance of a teacher facilitates a stronger connection with one's inner self, fostering an understanding of universal truths. This connection cultivates bhakti (devotion) towards the teacher, along with feelings of gratitude and love towards oneself and others.

Concept and Meaning of Yoga:

Excavation during the Indus Valley Civilization

Yoga traces its origins to the Vedas and was further developed into a specific philosophy by the sage Patanjali in his compilations known as the Yoga Sutra. Among the many texts and works on yoga, the Yoga Sutra holds particular significance.

The term "yoga" carries multiple interpretations, such as "to unite" or "to bind" and "to tie the strands of the mind together." While these interpretations may initially seem distinct, they ultimately convey the same message. The first interpretation, "to unite," pertains to the physical practice of yoga, while the second, "to tie the strands of the mind together," refers to the mental preparation before commencing the physical practice.

Furthermore, yoga can be understood as "to succeed in what was previously not achieved." For instance, successfully completing a previously challenging forward bend is an example of achieving success in yoga.

The Goal of Yoga:

Goal of Yoga

Individuals may have various objectives when they start yoga—some aim to become fit, while others wish to heal. Some seek increased flexibility, and others aspire to participate in yoga competitions. However, the ultimate goal of yoga is to transcend the limitations of the body and embark on a spiritual journey to connect with one's inner self. Regardless of the practitioner's goal, yoga equips them with the tools to achieve it.

The relationship between the body and mind is undeniable. The stress of modern daily life can take a toll on both, causing restlessness, anxiety, depression, agitation, and frustration. While asanas may initially appear to focus solely on the physical body, they also positively impact the brain's chemical balance, leading to improved mental well-being.

Yoga is not merely a physical practice. When done correctly, with proper alignment and technique, it can also unite the body and mind. Consistent practice brings positive changes to all areas of life, eliminating obstacles to good health and emotional stability. Through this practice, one can ultimately achieve liberation and self-realization—an ultimate goal for every person.

The Perfect Way to Health:

Health is not merely the absence of disease but rather the balance of all bodily systems. Like a river flowing with pure and fresh water, yoga poses bring balance to the respiratory, circulatory, nervous, digestive, excretory, hormonal, and reproductive systems. This bodily balance leads to mental peace and improved intellectual clarity. Additionally, the practice of yoga positively impacts how we manage our emotions.

In his book 'The Path to Holistic Health,' Sri B.K.S. Iyengar states that as people age, it becomes harder for them to perform physically vigorous exercises due to stiff joints and muscles that have lost tone. Therefore, practicing yoga at this stage of life is particularly beneficial. Yoga can help older individuals recuperate and resist illnesses, making it a valuable gift to them.

The Eight Limbs or Ashtanga Yoga:

8 petals of yoga

While many join yoga for its physical benefits, most people are unaware that yoga comprises eight limbs, or petals. A practitioner should understand what these eight limbs signify. The ancient sage Patanjali recognized the nature of humans and society during his time and simplified the practice of Ashtanga Yoga, beginning with a code of conduct and ending with the ultimate goal.

The eight limbs or petals are:

1. **Yama:** Yama details the moral principles to be observed in our daily lives. It has five principles. Ahimsa: non-violence. Satya: truthfulness. Asteya: freedom from greed for wealth. Aparigraha: freedom from desire. Brahmacharya: refraining from extramarital relations.

2. **Niyama:** Niyama deals with the positive current that is crucial for discipline, eliminating lethargy, and encouraging an inner desire to embrace the yogic way of life. It comprises five principles. Saucha: cleanliness. Santosha: contentment. Tapas: extreme self-discipline or austerity. Svadhyaya: self-study or self-introspection. Isvara Pranidhana: Devotion to God

3. **Asana:** By practicing asanas, one can develop the quality of self-discipline and raise their awareness of all things around them. At the same time, a person practicing an asana gets to focus their attention on their inner body to sharpen their intelligence.

4. **Pranayama:** Regulating the breath can eliminate negative thoughts and redirect one's energy inward, preparing the mind for Pratyahara.

5. **Pratyahara:** Pranayama practice leads to the withdrawal of the senses, which results in the detachment of the mind from desires and objects. This allows the mind to

move inward and be free from the influence of the senses, which is known as Pratyahara.

6. **Dharana:** Dharana is the act of directing one's attention to a single point of focus by utilizing the control over the senses gained through Pratyahara.

7. **Dhyana:** Prolonging a single point of focus results in Dhyana, where a yogi experiences peace and tranquility, is liberated from attachments, and perceives no distinctions between happiness and sorrow.

8. **Samadhi:** The state of total absorption is referred to as Samadhi. Quoting from Sri B.K.S. Iyengar's book, Sama means "level" or "alike," and adhi means "over" and "above." It also signifies the continuation of intelligence in a state of equilibrium.

PRANAYAMA

The practice of Pranayama is described as the fourth petal in "Ashtanga Yoga." Prana is the life force directly linked to breath and the mind. The ancient seers of India, who meditated deeply, practiced pranayama to unite breath with the mind.

According to "Ashtanga Yoga," Pranayama practice is the fourth petal. Prana is the life force directly linked to breath and the mind. When we look back at the ancient sages, they practiced pranayama to unite breath with the mind.

The word pranayama has two parts: prana and ayama, where prana means energy and ayama means the distribution of that energy. Ayama is even considered a three-dimensional aspect (vertical, horizontal, and cyclical extension). This means that when we practice pranayama, we learn to move energy vertically, horizontally, and cyclically throughout the entire body. This results in the activation of the quality of prana in the body at a higher frequency.

In yoga, prana is defined as the energy that animates the gross physical body, or "Sthula Roopa," and is responsible for its vitality. It is considered the subtle energy that gives life to the gross form.

Pranayama is a practice that aims to understand the flow of prana in the body. Breathing is a direct means of absorbing prana. The way we breathe impacts the flow of pranic energy, affecting our entire body and being. However, it is important to note that pranayama is not about deep or rapid breathing. Deep breathing often involves tensing facial muscles, which can lead to rigidity in the skull and chest. The use of external force during inhalation and exhalation could lead to stiffness in the lung tissues, impeding the flow of breath throughout the body.

प्रच्छर्दनविधारणाअभ्यां वा प्राणस्य ॥३४॥

prachchhardana-vidhāraṇa-ābhyāṁ vā prāṇasya ॥34॥

"By throwing out and restraining the breath, the mind may also be calmed."

The practice of controlled exhalation through the nostrils can also help calm the mind. The relationship between the mind and prana is closely connected. By gaining control over one, it is possible to also control the other. To regulate prana, one should practice breathing exercises. By doing so, the mind will also be pacified. Therefore, pranayama practices not only help to balance prana but also bring peace to the mind. This idea is supported by the Hatha Yoga Pradipika, which states that an imbalance in one will affect the other, and it is important to maintain balance to gain the maximum benefit.

Effects of Pranayama:

When the brain's nervous impulses are balanced and rhythmic, the brain functions properly, and its waves also become regular. The brain processes are closely connected to the brain and the nervous system, which are essential for the body. Irregular breathing can cause irregular impulses to the hypothalamus (a key part of the brain), resulting in disturbed impulses.

Irregular impulses from the heart can cause the organs in the chest, abdomen, and pelvis to respond in an arrhythmic or erratic manner, which can then send irregular impulses to the brain, leading to disharmony and imbalances. Therefore, whole-body dynamics can be regulated by paying attention to the breath and controlling it through techniques. Specifically, increasing the length of breath retention (kumbhaka) during pranayama practice can create a greater gap between the impulses of the nerves and their responses to the brain. Prolonging the retention period during pranayama practice can help reduce agitation in the mind.

Practicing asanas can remove obstacles that impede the free flow of prana. When practicing pranayama, it's important to observe the smooth flow of inhalation, exhalation, and retention of breath. According to the philosophy of yoga, a person's age is related to the total number of breaths they take in their lifetime. By practicing pranayama, one can alter their breathing pattern throughout the day.

For example, the average breath rate during different situations is:

- Sitting: 12 to 16 times per minute
- Sleeping: 30 to 35 times per minute
- Anger: 45 to 60 times per minute
- Relaxed: 2 to 3 times per minute.

As the number of breaths is reduced through practice, one may feel more peaceful and relaxed and experience an elevation in energy between the physical and mental bodies.

Sheethali Pranayama

Parts of Pranayama:

- Puraka (Inhalation)
- Rechaka (Exhalation)
- Kumbhaka (Retention)

Kumbhaka is further divided into three parts:

- Antar Kumbaka (retention post-inhalation)
- Bahya Kumbaka (retention post-exhalation)
- Kevala or Sahaja Kumbhaka (natural retention)

Sitakari Pranayama

Sadantha Pranayama

How does pranayama work?

Pranayama has two effects on the body:

1. **External:** Occurs in the lungs, where oxygen diffuses into the blood and carbon dioxide diffuses into the alveolar air.
2. **Internal:** Occurs in the tissues where oxygen diffuses out of the blood and carbon dioxide diffuses out of the cells.

On holding, hemoglobin present in the blood plus oxygen give rise to oxyhemoglobin, which enriches and energizes the whole body.

COMMONLY USED MUDRAS IN PRANAYAMA

Anjali or Namaskara Mudra

Chin Mudra in Padmasana

Mrigi Mudra

Nasika Or Nasagra or Vishnu Mudra

Shanmukhi Mudra

Dhyana or Bhairava Mudra

CHAKRAS

The word "chakra" means "wheel" or "circle." In yogic tradition, chakras are described as whirlpools of vital energy located at specified points in our body that regulate the flow of energy throughout the body. These chakras are associated with spiritual, emotional, psychological, and physical aspects of life and correspond to specific areas in the brain. They are typically dormant in most individuals. By focusing on the chakras during yoga practices, it is possible to stimulate the movement of energy through these chakras and actuate them.

The significant chakras, numbering seven, are situated at the pathway of SUSHUMNA, an energy channel that flows through the midst of the spinal cord. It begins at the perineum and ends at the crown of the head. The chakras are linked to a network of psychic channels called NADIS, which communicate with the nerves. Chakras are illustrated symbolically as lotus flowers, each having a specific number of petals and a particular color.

The lotus indicates the three phases through which the aspirant should pass in spiritual life: IGNORANCE, DESIRE, and ILLUMINATION. It constitutes spiritual growth from the lowest state of awareness to the highest state of consciousness. Blockages or imbalances in the chakras can cause health or psychological problems. These imbalances can be caused by factors such as lifestyle, environment, past experiences, and surroundings.

Each chakra is thought to have a different color element, and set of associated emotions and can be "opened" or "closed" depending on one's emotional and spiritual state. Imbalances or blockages in the chakras can lead to physical or emotional issues. Practicing meditation, yoga, and other spiritual practices is said to help balance and align the chakras.

Sahasrara Chakra (Crown Chakra):

Location		Crown of the Head
Meaning		Thousand Petal Lotus
Organs Associated		Crown of the Head, Brain, Nervous System, Lymphatic System
Gland		Pituitary Gland
Element		Light & Consciousness
Color		Violet / White
When Balanced		Understanding, Bliss, Spiritual, Open Minded, Unity, Wisdom, Strong Nervous System
When Imbalanced		Depression, Alienation, Confusion, Mental Disorders, Memory & Learning Problems, Broken, Fear

Ajna Chakra (Third Eye Chakra):

Location		Forehead
Meaning		Command
Organs Associated		Brain & Pituitary Gland
System		Nervous System
Element		Thought
Color		Indigo
When Balanced		Intuition, Visualization, Good Vision, Spiritual, Mental Strength, Bright Dreams
When Imbalanced		Lack of Intuition & Imagination, Eye Problems, Migraines, Panic, Fear, Nightmares

Vishuddhi Chakra (Throat Chakra):

Location	Throat
Meaning	Purifier
Organs Associated	Throat, Ear, Nose, Thyroid, Tongue
Gland	Thyroid
Element	Sound
Color	Light Blue
When Balanced	Truthful, Good Communication, Self-Expressive, Strong, Peaceful
When Imbalanced	Fear of Speaking, Arrogance, Unable to Listen, Throat Problems, Thyroid, Weak Voice, Lying, Shy

Anahata Chakra (Heart Chakra):

Location	Heart
Meaning	Unstruck Sound
Organs Associated	Thymus & Heart
Gland	Thymus
Element	Air
Color	Green
When Balanced	Unconditional Love, Wisdom, Pleasure, Patience, Joy, Kindness, Conscious Behavior, Decision Making
When Imbalanced	Asthma, Heart Disease, Lung Disease, High BP, Loneliness & Demanding

Manipura Chakra (Solar Plexus Chakra):

Location		Navel Region / Stomach
Meaning		Lustrous Gem
Organs Associated		Pancreas, Liver, Intestine & Digestive Organs
System		Digestive
Element		Fire
Color		Yellow
When Balanced		Will Power, Joy
When Imbalanced		Diabetes, Ulcers, Digestive Problems

Svadhisthana Chakra (Sacral Chakra):

Location		Lower Belly
Meaning		Well Established
Organs Associated		Muscles & Adrenals
System		Muscular
Element		Water
Color		Orange
When Balanced		Stability, Emotions, Decision, Self Confidence, Fertility, Patience, Prosperity, Creativity
When Imbalanced		Sexual Issues, Allergy, Irresponsible, Eating Disorder, Infertility, Shyness

Muladhara Chakra (Root Chakra):

Location		Base of the Spine
Meaning		Source
Organs Associated		Sex Glands, Bones, Blood Vertebral Column, Foot, Tooth
System		Skeletal
Element		Earth
Color		Red
When Balanced		Health, Stability, Security, Stamina & Endurance, Security, Grounded, Energetic, Stable, Healthy Eating
When Imbalanced		Insecurity, Fear, Anxiety, Constipation, Low Self Esteem, Over / Under Weight

INTRODUCTION TO AYURVEDA

Thousands of years ago, Ayurveda originated in India and was followed for a better healthcare system and medicine. "Ayur" means life, and "Veda" means science or knowledge, coined by the Sanskrit word to form the term Ayurveda. It can be interpreted as "the science of life" or "the knowledge of life." This holistic approach focuses on maintaining balance and well-being in the mind, body, and spirit.

According to Ayurveda, the three fundamental energies, or doshas—Vata, Pitta, and Kapha—need to be in balance for good health. These doshas represent different aspects of the mind and body, with Vata linked to movement, Pitta to metabolism, and Kapha to structure and lubrication. When these doshas are out of balance, it can lead to various health issues and illnesses. Ayurveda practitioners use a combination of different methods like herbal medicine, diet, yoga, meditation, and massage to help restore balance to the body and mind.

Ayurveda emphasizes the importance of preventive medicine and promoting healthy habits and lifestyle choices. A healthy diet, regular exercise, and stress management techniques are considered essential to maintaining balance in the body and mind. Additionally, Ayurveda practitioners may recommend seasonal cleansing programs, known as Panchakarma, to help purify the body and remove toxins.

Ayurveda is an integrated system of medicine that aims to treat the whole person rather than just their physical symptoms. It is gaining increasing popularity in western countries as people are looking for more natural, holistic alternatives to modern medicine. Today, Ayurveda is widely used to treat a variety of conditions, from chronic diseases to stress-related issues, as well as to promote overall well-being.

Ayurveda has its origins in the Vedic era, and according to Hindu mythology, Lord Brahma is considered the founder of Ayurveda, who imparted his knowledge to his son, Daksha Prajapathi. This knowledge was then passed on to the physicians of the gods, Ashwini Kumar and Bhaskar.

The Vedic teachings, such as the Rig Veda (3000–2500 BCE), Sama Veda (1200–1000 BCE), Yajur Veda (1200–1000 BCE), and Atharva Veda (1200–1000 BCE), were passed down orally from masters to disciples. The Upavedas, which are texts on applied knowledge, contain information on health and diseases, and the earliest of these texts is the Rig Veda, which also mentions medicinal plants. The Upavedas include the Gandharva Veda (art forms such as music and dance), the Dhanur Veda (archery and warfare), the Ayurveda (knowledge of health and life), and the Sthapatya Veda (architecture and engineering).

The history of Ayurveda can be traced back to around 5000 years ago in India and is well documented in ancient texts called Sutras. The three main texts of Ayurveda are the Charaka Samhita, the Sushruta Samhita, and the Ashtanga Hridayam.

Charaka is said to have been a court physician for Kushana King Kanishka in the 1st century AD. The Charaka Samhita was later revised by Acharya Dridhabala in the 4th century. Sushruta, a surgeon in the Gupta court, wrote the Sushruta Samhita, which was later revised by Nagarjuna in the 6th century. Vagbhata is considered one of the most influential writers, scientists, and doctors in Ayurveda. He lived in Sind and was a disciple of Charaka. He wrote the famous Ashtanga Hridayam, a concise version of the Charaka and Sushruta Samhitas, containing 7000 sutras. Vagbhata stated that 85% of diseases can be cured without a doctor, and only 15% require a doctor's attention.

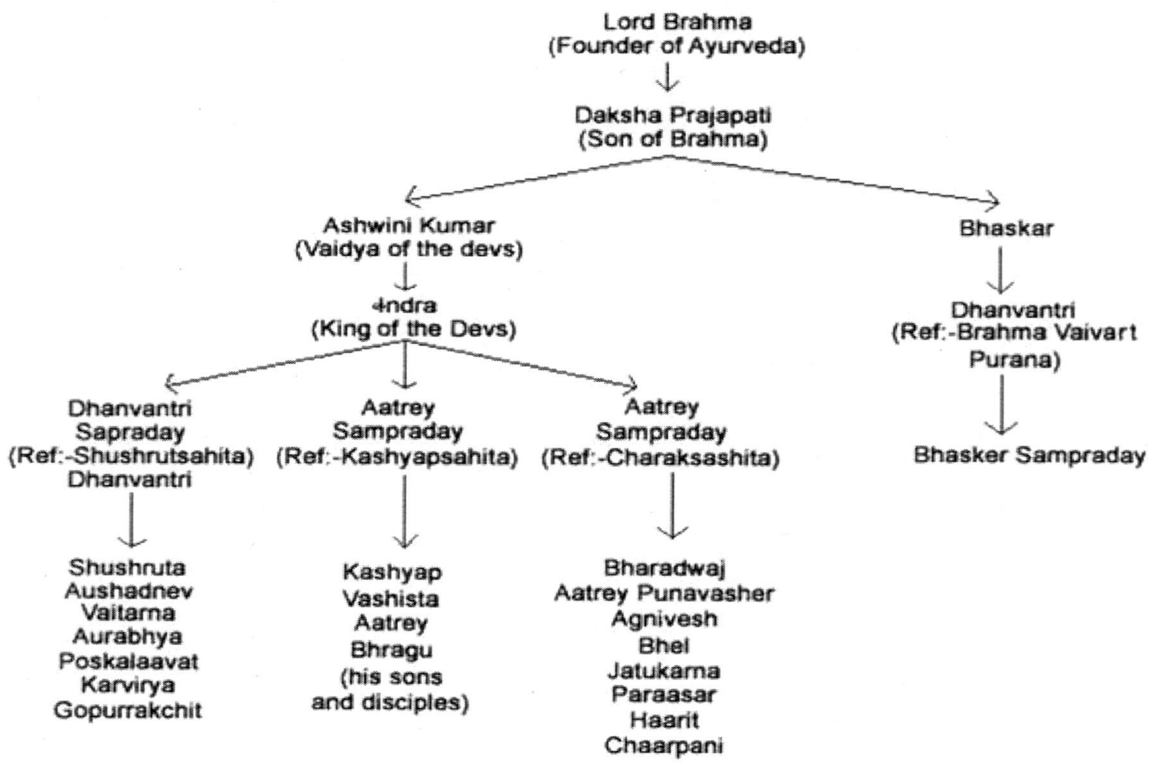

According to Ayurveda, the main aim of this science is to maintain one's health to achieve wellness by preventing illness and managing disease and ailments to regain good health. The renowned Ayurvedic surgeon and teacher, Acharya Sushruta (1200 BCE–600 BCE), defined health as a balance of the Tridosha, Agni, Mala, and Dhatu for the physical aspect and the Indriya and Manas for the mental aspect.

Ayurveda is divided into eight branches, collectively referred to as Ashtanga Ayurveda. The word "Ashtanga" means "eight," and yoga, the sister science of Ayurveda, also has eight branches.

The eight branches of Ayurveda are:

1. **Kaya Chikitsa:** This branch deals with general medicine, including the diagnosis, treatment, and prevention of various illnesses and conditions.

2. **Bala Chikitsa:** This branch focuses on the treatment of pediatrics and the care of children's health.

3. **Graha Chikitsa:** This branch deals with the treatment of various types of mental and neurological disorders, such as psychosis, depression, and epilepsy.

4. **Shayla Chikitsa:** This branch deals with surgery and the treatment of injuries, including the use of surgical instruments and techniques.

5. **Salakya Chikitsa:** This branch deals with the treatment of disorders related to the head, such as the eyes, ears, nose, and throat.

6. **Damstra Chikitsa:** This branch deals with toxicology, including the treatment of poisonings and the use of various types of antidotes.

7. **Jara Chikitsa:** This branch deals with geriatrics, including the treatment of age-related diseases and the care of the elderly.

8. **Vrishya Chikitsa:** This branch deals with the treatment of infertility and sexual disorders and also includes the promotion of overall reproductive health.

These branches of Ayurveda are interrelated and complement each other, providing a holistic approach to health and wellness. They are still being studied and developed today and are being used in many forms of treatment.

Ayurvedic Philosophy:

Ayurveda describes Shad Darshan (the Six Philosophies of Life) as the vision or realization of the self. These are:

1. **Sankhya:** Sankhya, meaning "right knowledge" or "numbers," is a philosophy that recognizes 25 categories or principles.

2. **Nyaya Darshan:** Nyaya Darshan, also known as the Nyaya school of Indian philosophy, is focused on the principles of logic and reasoning. The word "Nyaya" means "rules," "method," or "judgment."

3. **Vaisheshika:** The Vaisheshika philosophy closely follows the Nyaya system and is

often considered its twin philosophy. This system recognizes seven Padarthas, or categories, which include substance, quality, action, generality, particularity, the relation of inference, and non-existence.

4. **Poorva Mimansa:** Poorva Mimansa is a philosophy that emphasizes thorough investigation and rational justification for the performance of rituals. The principle of Apoorva ensures the desired outcome of these rituals. The ultimate goal of human life, according to Mimansa, is to attain a transcendent state, such as heaven.

5. **Yoga:** The Yoga Darshana, as represented by the Yoga Sutras, was expounded by Maharishi Patanjali. The Yoga Sutras are considered the foundational text of yoga and outline an Ashtanga system of eight limbs. The Sutras are divided into four chapters, or Padas, which include:

   - Samadhi Pada: 51 Sutras
   - Sadhana Pada: 55 Sutras
   - Vibhuti Pada: 55 Sutras
   - Kaivalya Pada: 34 Sutras

   Each Pada delves into different aspects of yoga, from reaching the state of Samadhi to the practices of Sadhana to the attainment of supernatural abilities and ultimate liberation, respectively.

6. **Vedantic Philosophy:** Vedantic philosophy is not attributed to a single founder but rather developed through various schools of thought by different teachers. The three main schools are Advaita, Visishtadvaita, and Dvaita. Adi Shankaracharya is credited with promoting the Advaita system, Ramanujacharya with creating the Visishtadvaita system, and Madhavacharya as the leader of the Dvaita system. It is important to note that while all three teachers recognized the authority of the Vedas, their interpretations of the Brahma Sutra varied.

Core Principles of Ayurveda:

Ayurveda is an ancient Indian system of medicine based on the concept of balance and harmony between the body, mind, and spirit. The core principles of Ayurveda are:

1. **Tridosha:** Ayurveda posits that the body is made up of three fundamental energies, or doshas: vata, pitta, and kapha. These doshas govern the body's metabolic and physiological processes, and an imbalance can lead to illness.

2. **Prakriti:** Prakriti is the unique combination of doshas that each individual is born with, determining their physical and mental characteristics.

3. **Agni:** Agni is the body's metabolic fire responsible for digestion, assimilation, and metabolism. A healthy Agni is crucial for overall health.

4. **Ama:** Ama is a toxic by-product of poor digestion and metabolism, considered the root cause of many illnesses and a precursor to disease development.

5. **Dinacharya And Ritucharya:** Dinacharya (daily routine) and Ritucharya (seasonal routine) are crucial principles. Daily routines maintain overall health, while seasonal routines adapt to changing seasons and maintain body balance.

6. **The Six Tastes:** Ayurveda recognizes six tastes: sweet, sour, salty, spicy (pungent), bitter, and astringent. Each taste has a unique effect on the body and mind, and a balance is necessary for optimal health.

7. **The Five Elements:** Ayurveda believes the universe comprises five elements: earth, water, fire, air, and ether. These elements are present in the body, influencing health.

These core principles form the foundation of Ayurveda, and understanding and applying them are essential for maintaining health and well-being.

Let us learn more about Tridoshas:

- **Vata: Air and Ether**

Vata is the energy of movement and is primarily composed of the elements of air and space. It is more likely to become imbalanced during the summer and rainy seasons, making it important to adjust your diet and lifestyle accordingly. Vata also controls the elimination of waste and plays a role in childbirth.

When Vata is balanced, individuals tend to be creative, energetic, and positive. When it becomes unbalanced, they may experience restlessness, anxiety, and an unstable mood. They may also be sensitive to colds, have difficulty sleeping, and exhibit irregular sleep patterns. Common vata disorders include constipation, flatulence, nerve disorders, pneumonia, arthritis, mental confusion, and dry skin.

As Vata is characterized as being cold, light, dry, subtle, rough, flowing, and clear, an excess of these qualities can lead to imbalances. To balance Vata, it is important to avoid excessive exposure to cold, take warm baths, use humidifiers, and apply moisture to the skin. Additionally, one should consume warm meals, avoid cold and raw foods, get enough rest, and maintain a regular daily routine.

- **Pitta: Fire and Water**

Pitta is the energy of digestion and metabolism and is composed of the elements of fire and water. It is commonly described as hot, light, sharp, oily, liquid, and mobile. The season of Sharad, or autumn, just after the monsoon, is known to be the Pitta season. People with balanced Pitta tend to have warm bodies, are athletic, sharp, intelligent, motivated, and goal-oriented. They have good digestion and a strong metabolism.

When Pitta becomes imbalanced, individuals may become impatient, always hungry, easily agitated, and aggressive. To balance Pitta, people should avoid extreme heat and focus on maintaining a balance between work and life. When Pitta is in excess, it can lead to diseases such as fevers, skin rashes, ulcerations, and inflammations. They should consume sweet, cooling, and bitter foods and avoid excessive oil, sour, salty, and pungent foods, as they are intolerant by nature.

- **Kapha: Earth and Water**

Kapha is the energy of lubrication, and when balanced, individuals have good strength, endurance, and stamina. They are stable and grounded, with smooth and oily skin. This dosha tends to accumulate during the winter season and can become imbalanced during the spring. As it is hibernation season, individuals tend to gain weight easily and have a slow metabolism. They tend to have thick skin and well-developed bodies. People with balanced Kapha are calm, patient, trustworthy, caring, and empathetic. When unbalanced, they may be sluggish and lethargic and have a higher risk for heart disease, depression, and diabetes.

To balance Kapha, individuals should consume a well-balanced diet with more bitter, astringent, and pungent tastes. They should avoid sweets, dairy products, and fried or greasy foods. Kapha-dominant individuals should consume less grain than Pitta or Vata and consume more raw vegetables if they can digest them. They should stay active, avoid heavy foods, cold, and icy foods and drinks, and maintain a healthy and active lifestyle.

Srotas:

Srotas, in Ayurvedic medicine, refers to the channels or pathways in the body through which various bodily fluids, such as blood, lymph, and plasma, flow. These channels also serve as pathways for the movement of nutrients, hormones, and other substances throughout the body. The concept of srotas is important in Ayurveda because it is believed that the functioning of the srotas is crucial for maintaining overall health and preventing disease.

In Ayurveda, there are said to be 14 main srotas in the body, including those for the circulatory, respiratory, digestive, excretory, and reproductive systems. Each srota is closely connected to one or more of the doshas (Vata, Pitta, and Kapha) and can become blocked or unbalanced due to an imbalance in the doshas. When a srota is blocked or unbalanced, it can lead to health issues, including pain, inflammation, and disease.

To maintain the health of the srotas, Ayurveda recommends a variety of methods, including diet, herbal remedies, and lifestyle changes. For example, eating a balanced diet, avoiding foods that are too cold, hot, or heavy, and getting enough rest can help to keep the srotas functioning properly. Herbs such as ginger, turmeric, and licorice can also be used to support the health of the srotas. Additionally, certain yoga poses, pranayama techniques, and other practices can be used to strengthen the srotas and improve overall health.

Cleansing programs such as Panchakarma, which remove impurities from the body and improve the functioning of the srotas, can also be beneficial in maintaining overall health.

In conclusion, srotas are essential channels in the body that are responsible for the flow of bodily fluids and the movement of nutrients, hormones, and other substances. The concept of srotas plays an important role in Ayurveda, as the health of these channels is believed to be crucial for maintaining overall health and preventing disease. By following a balanced diet, using herbal remedies, practicing yoga and pranayama, and undergoing Panchakarma, one can maintain the health of the srotas, improve overall health, and prevent diseases.

Ayurvedic Recommendations for a Healthy Lifestyle:

To maintain balance in the doshas and srotas, Ayurveda recommends incorporating a morning routine for improved health. This routine includes:

1. **Excreting Waste Material:** To remove toxins, one should scrape the tongue, preferably using a copper scraper.
2. **Brushing The Teeth And Oil Pulling:** Engage in oil pulling to remove toxins and maintain oral hygiene.
3. **Applying Nasya Oil:** Apply 2 drops of Nasya oil to each nostril to clear the sinuses and lubricate the nasal passages.
4. **Medicated Smoking Of Plants:** Perform medicated smoking three times per nostril.
5. **Abhyanga (Oil Massage):** Stimulate the lymphatic system through a rejuvenating oil massage.
6. **Dry Brushing:** Remove dead skin cells through the practice of dry brushing.
7. **Yoga Practice:** Include Sun Salutation (Surya Namaskar) to open body channels, ignite the internal fire, and prepare muscles for the day.
8. **Specific Yoga Poses:** Practice yoga poses tailored to benefit individual doshas under the guidance of a therapeutic yoga teacher.
9. **Pranayama:** Engage in pranayama to cleanse the lungs, enhance cognitive function, reduce stress, and improve mental strength.
10. **Taking A Bath:** Follow the morning routine with a refreshing bath.
11. **Having Breakfast**: Conclude the routine with a nutritious breakfast.

It's important to note that regardless of any irregularities in the doshas, one can perform Surya Namaskar while paying attention to alignment and modifications needed to reap the benefits of the practice. Improving the range of mobility, ensuring joint safety during asanas, and concentrating on inhalation and exhalation with each pose are essential to maximizing the benefits of the practice.

FOOD & NUTRITION

How do we gain the energy we require? What fuels our system to work efficiently? What provides us with the nourishment we need to stay strong and healthy? The answer is the food we eat.

Good nutrition is crucial and serves as the first line of defense against diseases. Food is a significant aspect of life, and the choice of food plays a vital role in strengthening, maintaining, rejuvenating, and healing the body.

Food is divided into micro- and macronutrients, further categorized into carbohydrates, fats, proteins, vitamins, and minerals.

Our body requires all nutrients in specific amounts to function efficiently.

Nutrient deficiency can have a negative impact, resulting in malnourishment, weakness, anemia, scurvy, osteoporosis, etc.

On the other hand, overeating can lead to weight gain, causing issues like PCOS, diabetes, hypertension, etc.

Mindful eating is crucial for maintaining a healthy balance.

Following a healthy lifestyle consisting of yoga and a diet rich in fiber, protein, vitamins, and sufficient carbohydrates works wonders for the body and mind. Fruits, vegetables, dairy products, and nuts are essential for our daily nutritional needs.

According to ancient Indian Ayurveda, there are three types of food groups.

Types of Food:

Sattvic Food: The term Sattvic is derived from the Sanskrit word Sattva, meaning purity. The Sattvic diet comprises fresh food that is light and easily digestible at normal or room temperature. Traditionally, the food is consumed after sunrise and before sunset. Consumption of Sattvic food is thought to increase energy, happiness, calmness, and mental clarity. Some fruits, vegetables, spices, grains, and nuts that can be consumed in a Sattvic diet include:

Fruits	Apples, bananas, guavas etc.
Vegetables	Spinach, carrots, coriander, potato etc.
Spices & Stimulants	Cinnamon, asafetida, turmeric.
Grains & Pulses	Rice, barley, dal, sprouts etc.
Nuts & Seeds	Coconut almonds, pumpkin seeds etc.

Rajasic Food: The term Rajasic comes from the Sanskrit word Rajas, signifying passion and activity. Rajasic foods are hot, salty, and pungent. Some fruits, vegetables, spices, grains, and nuts that can be consumed in a Rajasic diet include:

Fruits	Apples, bananas, guavas etc.
Vegetables	Cauliflower, broccoli, spinach, tamarind, onions, garlic etc.
Spices & Stimulants	Chili, pepper, coffee, tea etc.
Grains & Pulses	Millets, buckwheat, corn.
Nuts & Seeds	Coconut, almonds, pumpkin seeds etc.

Rajasic food also includes red meat, alcohol, tobacco, chocolates, and refined sugar.

This type of food stimulates and over-excites the body and mind. Consuming excess oil, spice, ginger, onion, garlic, refined sugar, etc. from a Rajasic diet can lead to disruption of mind-body equilibrium. The mind becomes restless and doesn't switch off even during rest or sleep. It can also lead to anxiety, anger, and hate. This imbalance can be reversed by eating in balance with Sattvic food.

Tamasic Food: The term Tamasic comes from the Sanskrit word Tamas, meaning darkness. Tamasic foods include anything that is aged, inclusive of alcohol or fermented. Some fruits, vegetables, spices, grains, and nuts that can be consumed in a Tamasic diet include:

Fruits	Watermelons, avocados, plums etc.
Vegetables	Mushrooms, pumpkins, onions, garlic etc.
Spices & Stimulants	None
Grains & Pulses	Wheat, rice, refined grains, urad dal, black dal etc.

Nuts & Seeds	Chia seeds, seeds exposed to light etc.

Tamasic foods also include meat, fish, and highly processed foods like bread, cakes, maida, etc. They cloud the mind, lower our resistance to disease, and promote negative emotions. Tamasic foods block the flow of energy, making the person lethargic.

In addition, overeating or reheating leftover or stale food that was once Sattvic can also turn it into Tamasic food.

Conclusion:

To maintain a healthy lifestyle, it is best to consume Sattvic food. However, moderate consumption of Rajasic and Tamasic foods is advised for balanced nutrition.

Essential Vitamins & Minerals:

Vitamins / Minerals	Ailments	Found in
Calcium	Osteoporosis, high blood pressure, hyperthyroidism, perimenopause, etc.	Broccoli, dairy products, tofu, etc.
Folate	Osteoporosis, rheumatoid arthritis, heart disease, etc.	Avocados, cabbage family, citrus fruits, beans, beets, lentils, etc.
Iron	Anemia, immune deficiency, etc.	Lentils, spinach, peas, apricots, etc.
Magnesium	Asthma, constipation, diabetes, high blood pressure, etc.	Seeds, nuts, tofu, spinach, avocados, etc.
Selenium	Hypothyroidism, eye problem, asthma, etc.	Nuts, seeds, whole grains, etc.
Vitamin B6	Hypothyroidism, pms, stress, depression, heart disease, anemia, etc.	Sweet potato, peanuts, banana, peas, potato, etc.
Vitamin B12	Anemia, mental impairment, headache, fatigue, etc.	Dairy products, fortified breakfast cereal, etc.
Vitamin C	Asthma, headache, diabetes, high blood pressure, arthritis, osteoporosis, etc.	Berries, cabbage family, citrus fruits, tomatoes, etc.
Vitamin E	Hyperthyroidism, osteoarthritis, rheumatoid arthritis, etc.	Nuts, seeds, peanuts, pumpkin, red bell pepper, etc.
Zinc	Bronchitis, cold, hypothyroidism, sinusitis, etc.	Legumes, seeds, nuts, dairy products, etc.

SURYA NAMASKAR (SUN SALUTATIONS)

Surya Namaskar (Sun Salutation) is a sequence of 12 graceful and powerful yoga poses, traditionally performed as a gesture of respect to the sun. The name is derived from Sanskrit roots, with "Surya" meaning "Sun" and "Namaskar" meaning "Greetings" or "Salutations." It embodies a fundamental element of yoga, evident in the set of asanas (poses) incorporated into one complete round. Therefore, it is often referred to as “Yogasara,” signifying the "Power of union."

Surya Namaskar is best practiced before other asanas or as a warm-up exercise preceding a broader yoga practice. Although not explicitly mentioned in textbooks, the benefits of practicing Surya Namaskara are immense. The practice also serves as an opportunity to express gratitude to the Sun for sustaining life on Mother Earth, emphasizing a holistic approach.

Regular practice of Surya Namaskar impacts the entire body, including organs such as the lungs, liver, heart, chest, stomach, intestines, and throat. The synchronization of breath with each movement brings clarity to the mind by infusing fresh, oxygenated blood into the brain, enhancing focus, awareness, and skin health. It promotes proper bowel function and cleanses the digestive tract, contributing to the balance of the tri-doshas in Ayurveda: Vata, Pitta, and Kapha. Recognized as the ultimate practice, Surya Namaskar makes practitioners mentally and physically strong. It aids in weight regulation and sugar level control and supports skin and hair health. Its positive effects on the endocrine glands assist in balancing the transition from childhood to adolescence in children.

Steps To Perform:

1. Pranamasana (Namaskara Mudra):

- Stand upright with the feet together, toes in, and heels slightly apart, arms resting by the side of the legs.
- Raise the hands and join the palms together in front of the chest in Namaskar Mudra.
- Breathe normally.
- This pose enhances concentration and brings calmness to prepare for the steps to follow.

Pranamasana
(Namaskara Mudra)

2. Urdhva Veekshana (Upward Gazing Pose):

- Breathe in.
- Raise and stretch the hands above the head, separating the hands to shoulder width, drop the head slightly, bend the upper trunk backward, and gaze up towards the ceiling.

Urdhva Veekshana (Upward Gazing Pose)

3. Hasta Pada Asana (Forward Fold):

- Breath Out
- Fold forward and place the palms by the sides of the feet.
- Do not strain.
- Maintain the knees straight.
- Contract the abdomen to expel the air from the lungs.

Hasta Pada Asana (Forward Fold)

4. Eka Pada Prasaransana (One Leg Stretch Pose):

- Breathe in.
- With the hands by the sides of the feet, take the right leg back, placing the foot flat on the mat.
- Stretch the upper body and widen the chest, slightly tilt the head, and gaze upwards towards the ceiling.

Urdhva Veekshana (Upward Gazing Pose)

5. Adho Mukha Dandasana (High Plank Pose):

- Breathe out.
- Now take the left leg back and place it by the side of the right leg.
- Do not allow the trunk to drop down.

Adho Mukha Dandasana (High Plank Pose)

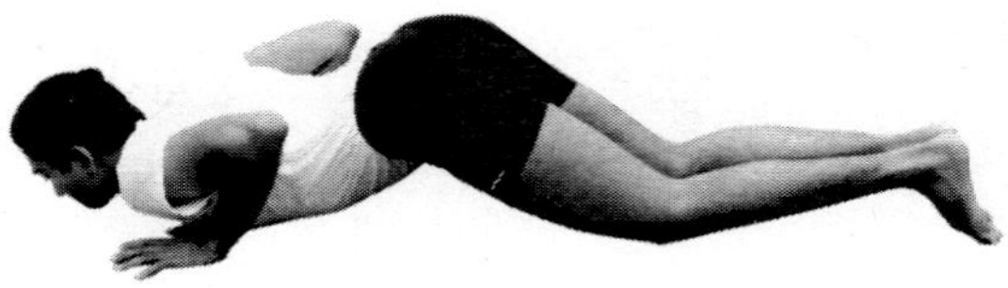

Saashtanga Namaskara
(Salute With Eight Limbs Pose)

6. Saashtanga Namaskara (Salute With Eight Limbs Pose):

- Hold the Breath (Bahya Kumbhaka)
- With the hands and legs already in contact with the mat, gently drop the knees, chest, chin, or forehead on the mat, bringing the eight parts of the body into the salute position.
- Maintain the buttocks lifted in this position.
- Do not bring the abdomen into contact with the mat.

7. Bhujangasana (Cobra Pose):

- Breathe in.
- With the feet flat on the mat and the hands by the side of the chest, raise the chest and shoulders, then try to straighten the elbows and arch the back to Cobra pose.
- Drop the head slightly to gaze upward.
- Try not to raise the thighs.

Bhujangasana (Cobra Pose)

Parvatasana
(Mountain or Inverted V Pose)

8. Parvatasana (Mountain/Inverted V Pose):

- Breathe out.
- Come up on the toes, lift the knees above the ground, raise the buttocks as high as possible towards the ceiling, and place the feet completely on the mat, forming a mountain pose.

9. Ek Pada Prasaranasana (One Leg Stretch Pose):

- Breathe in.
- Bring the right leg forward in between the palms.
- Breathe in.
- Stretch the upper body and widen the chest,

Ek Pada Prasaranasana
(One Leg Stretch Pose)

slightly tilt the head, and gaze upwards towards the ceiling.

10. Hasta Pada Asana (Forward Fold):

- Breathe out.
- Join the left leg with the right leg.
- Bend forward.
- Straighten the legs with the knees straight.
- Contract the abdomen to expel the air from the lungs.

Hasta Pada Asana
(Forward Fold)

11. Urdhva Veekshana (Upward Gazing Pose):

- Breathe in.
- Raise and stretch the hands above the head, separating the hands to shoulder width.
- Drop the head slightly, bend the upper trunk backwards, and gaze up towards the ceiling.

Urdhva Veekshana (Upward Gazing Pose)

12. Prayer Pose (Namaskara Mudra):

- Breathe out.
- Come back to Namaskar Mudra.
- Breathe normally.

Prayer Pose (Namaskara Mudra)

Who can practice surya namaskara?

Surya Namaskar can be practiced by anyone, irrespective of age, gender, and religion. However, under certain conditions, such as pregnancy, high blood pressure, lumbar or cervical issues, back pain, knee pain, and so on, it is advisable to practice under the guidance of a therapeutic yoga teacher. They can modify the practice according to the individual's requirements or ailments.

Who cannot practice surya namaskara?

It is advised not to practice Surya Namaskar during menstruation. Individuals who have just recovered from a serious ailment may have weakened energy; hence, it is better not to practice immediately. However, a therapeutic yoga teacher can provide a modified version of Surya Namaskar for people with various health conditions. Therefore, it is recommended to practice under the supervision of a therapeutic yoga teacher.

STRESS

Stress can be defined as the body's response to pressure. Various distinct events or circumstances can cause stress. Most of the time, it is triggered by something unexpected—fear, new experiences, or when we feel we have little control over a situation.

When we are stressed, our body produces stress hormones that trigger a fight-or-flight response and activate our immune system. This helps us respond spontaneously to dangerous situations. Once the stress event is over, usually the stress hormones normalize. However, too much stress can cause negative effects, and in the long term, this can affect our physical and mental health.

Managing stress differs from individual to individual. Our ability to manage stress can depend on an individual's genetic makeup, early life events, personality, and socioeconomic situation.

Some types of stress include:

- **Acute Stress:** Very short-term, triggered by either negative or positive events, such as losing or breaking items.
- **Chronic Stress:** Long-term stress, such as financial crises or failed marital issues.
- **Episodic Acute Stress:** Frequent occurrences of acute stress.
- **Eustress:** Eustress is a positive form of stress that has beneficial effects on health.

According to Ayurveda, stress is known as sahasa. Stress affects the body's immunity (Ojahksaya), decreasing its fighting capacity against diseases. Stress can be considered a primary cause of many problems. According to Charaka Samhita, Sahasa adversely affects the body, and thus, the body should be well protected by taking adequate care of the three sub-pillars of life: diet, sleep, and celibacy (Traya Upastambhithi: ahara, nidra, and brahmacharya).

Avoiding causative factors is the first rule in preventing disease, but one must also be self-aware to identify the stress response and avoid it. Hence, self-awareness and listening to your body's intelligence are the second rule for preventing disease.

However, stress can be experienced if there is an imbalance in any of the three doshas (Vata, Pitta, and Kapha) or a combination of them. It can also be a decreased state of formation of the dhatu or an occlusion in the movement of one of the doshas. Ayurveda categorizes emotions according to dosha predominance:

- Worry, anxiety, and fear will increase the dosha of vata in the body.
- Impatience, anger, and frustration will imbalance pitta in the body.
- Depression, lack of energy, and laziness will imbalance kapha in the body.

Causes:

There might be a significant unpleasant incident that has caused stress, or it can be due to provoking small pressures that ultimately build up to cause stress. However, some of the common reasons that cause stress are:

- Worrying.
- Uncertainty.
- Not having control over the outcome of a situation.
- Facing big changes.
- Overwhelming responsibilities.
- Being under lots of pressure.
- No change in life, no activities, not having enough work—pandemic (like coronavirus).

Feelings of stress are primarily triggered by things happening in an individual's life, and the reasons may vary from person to person. Some of the reasons include:

- **Personal:** Injury, pregnancy, long-term health problems.
- **Friends and Family:** Going through a breakup or getting divorced, getting married, difficult relationships with parents, siblings, children, friends, or losing a loved one.
- **Employment and Study:** Long-term unemployment, losing a job, starting a new job, exams.

- **Housing:** Debt, poverty, worry about money.
- **Social Factors:** Experiencing discrimination like racism and transphobia, and living in areas with poor access to medical care and transport.

Due to poor management of stress, some of the consequences are stress cardiomyopathy (acute stress) (broken heart syndrome), heart attack, hypertension, diabetes, obesity, mood disorders, insomnia, etc.

Symptoms:

Some of the signs of stress include:

- Difficulty concentrating, anxiety symptoms, trouble remembering, and worrisome behavior.
- Getting agitated, frustrated, and irritated.
- Symptoms of high blood pressure.
- Changes in the menstrual cycle and decreased libido.
- Affecting daily activities, not taking proper care of health.
- Poor coping mechanisms, like depending on drugs and alcohol.

Diagnosis:

Stress is extremely subjective and is not measurable with tests. Only the person experiencing it can say how severe the stress is. However, when consulting a medical professional, they may conduct a series of tests, which may include:

- Personal and family health history.
- Blood and urine tests and other assessments.
- Investigations.
- Treadmill test.
- Electrocardiogram.

Yogic Intervention:

Yoga inspires mental and physical relaxation, promoting flexibility, relieving tension, reducing pain, and easing stress and anxiety. Practicing yoga asanas regularly helps release physical blockages in muscles, emotions, and tension. It also promotes the release of endorphins, providing a sense of well-being and boosting moods, aiding in dealing positively with stressful situations.

Along with asana practice, pranayama helps focus on the present moment, improving awareness, focus, and centering the mind, thereby soothing the mind and body and relieving stress. As we become more mindful of our present sensations, emotions, and thoughts, it becomes easier to let go of uneasiness and develop feelings of love, joy, and serenity.

Case Study:

Subjective: Mr. Avinash (name changed) from Bangalore, a college student and a badminton player, was referred to us by his aunt, who had been our student for many years. He started losing interest in studies, badminton, and life and began having suicidal tendencies.

Objective: He was diagnosed with stress and depression.

Assessment: He was prescribed medication after counseling by a well-known psychiatrist in Bangalore. Although the medicine worked momentarily, his attitude did not change over a period of time.

Plan: His aunt advised his father to bring him to our yoga center in Mysore for yoga therapy. He came with his father, and we discussed his issues in detail. Afterward, we planned a yoga therapy program for 10 days initially, which was later extended to 3 months, totaling 25 classes. During this period, he shuffled between Bangalore and Mysore.

He continues to practice yoga regularly, about 3 to 4 times a week, and has started to feel significantly better and happier. Over time, he has also regained interest in life and education, excelling in the field of badminton and even winning a shield in one of his college competitions.

- **Surya Namaskar (Sun Salutations):**

Regular practice of Surya Namaskars can be beneficial.

- **Asanas (Yoga Postures):**

The following are some postures that are helpful in managing stress:

1. Parivritta Tadasana (Revolved Mountain Pose):

Steps To Perform:

1. Stand in Tadasana with the feet mat-width apart.
2. Bring the right hand to the left shoulder, inhale, lengthen the spine, and as you exhale, twist the torso to the left, bringing the left hand behind the back close to the right hip.
3. Stay and breathe for 30 seconds to 1 minute.
4. Come back to Tadasana and repeat on the other side.

Joint Actions:

- Lateral rotation of the spine.
- Posterior-inferior glide, retraction of the scapula.
- Flexion of the elbow front.
- Pronation of the forearm.
- Supination of the rear arm and wrist in a neutral position.
- Hips are neutral, with knees in extension.
- Lateral rotation of the cervical spine.

Main Muscle Actions:

- During rotation, the external oblique, rectus abdominis, and lumbar multifidus muscles act contralaterally, whereas the latissimus dorsi, internal oblique, and transversus abdominis muscles act ipsilaterally at the lumbar spine.

- At the cervical level: semispinalis cervicis muscles, multifidus scalene muscles, splenius capitis muscles, and sternocleidomastoid muscles.

Things To Focus On:

- Keep the shoulders over the hips and the hips in line with the ankles.
- Engage the large muscles in the standing thighs and lower leg to give the body a stable base.
- Draw the navel in and engage the core, chest, neck, and shoulders, and then twist the upper body.

Things To Be Cared For:

- Those who are suffering from severe headaches, back injuries, hip injuries, and shoulder injuries, have recently had any surgery on the back or waist, or have spinal column ailments on the lower vertebrae should not practice this asana.
- Those who are suffering from high or low blood pressure should do this asana under the supervision of a therapeutic yoga teacher.

2. Urdhva Baddhanguliyasana in Tadasana (Fingers Interlocked Over the Head Pose):

Steps To Perform:

1. Stand in Tadasana, inhale, lengthen the spine, interlock the fingers, and extend the arms over the head, turning the palms up towards the ceiling.
2. Stay here and breathe for 30 seconds to 1 minute.
3. Exhale, release the arms, and come back to Tadasana.

Joint Actions:

- Neutral position of the spine.
- Extension of the elbow.
- Flexion of the shoulders.
- Supination and wrist extension.
- Hip in neutral.
- Extension of the knee and ankle in a neutral position.

Main Muscle Actions:

- Retractors and flexors of the shoulder muscles.
- Erector spinae muscles.
- Extensors and a group of forearms.

Things To Focus On:

- Maintain the alignment of Tadasana throughout the pose.
- Keep the shoulders over the hips and the hips in line with the ankles.
- Engage the large muscles in the thighs and lower legs to give the body a stable base.
- Focus on lifting the arms and shoulders to expand the ribs.

Things To Be Cared For:

- People with neck or shoulder pain should practice yoga under the supervision of a therapeutic yoga teacher.
- People with headaches, insomnia, exhaustion, or low blood pressure should avoid this asana.

➢ Pregnant women should widen their stance as much as necessary to feel stable.

Tadasana in Urdhva Badda Hasta
Variation 1

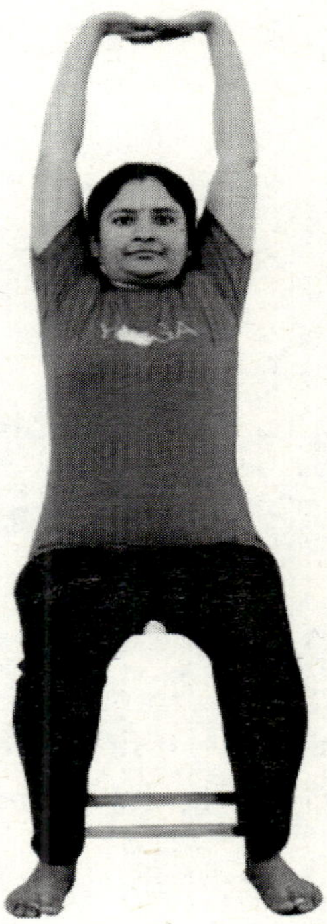

Tadasana in Urdhva Badda Hasta
Variation 2

3. Urdhva Baddha Hasta Dandasana (Bound Hands Overhead Staff Pose):

Steps To Perform:

1. Sit in Dandasana.
2. Inhale, lengthen the spine, stretch the arms over the head, and interlock the fingers with the palms facing the ceiling.
3. Stay here and breathe for 30 seconds to 1 minute.
4. Come back to Dandasana.

Joint Actions:

- Neutral position of the spine.
- External rotation and abduction of the glenohumeral joint.
- Internal rotation of the hip.
- Extension of the knee.
- Dorsiflexion of the ankle.

Main Muscle Actions:

- Retractors and flexor muscles of the shoulder.
- Erector spinae muscles.
- Contraction of gastrocnemius muscles.
- The extensor muscle group of the forearm.

Things To Focus On:

- Engage the adductor muscles of the thighs to internally rotate the hips.
- Focus on keeping the wrists over the elbows, the elbows over the shoulders, the shoulders over the hips, and the hips in line with the ankles.
- Point the toes inward to feel the stretch on the calves and hamstrings.
- Keep the neck neutral and gaze straight ahead without straining the neck.
- Focus on drawing the navel in towards the tailbone by engaging the core muscles.

Things To Be Cared For:

- People with neck pain, shoulder pain, or lower back pain should avoid this pose or practice under the supervision of a therapeutic yoga teacher.

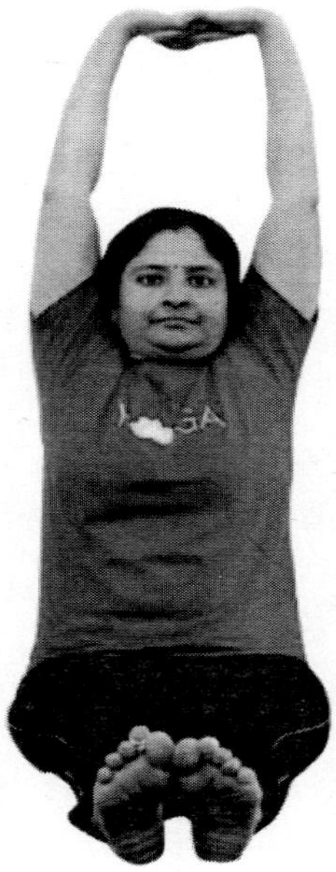

Urdhva Badda Hasta Dandasana Variation 1

Urdhva Badda Hasta Dandasana Variation 2

4. Janu Sirsasana (Head to Knee Pose):

Steps To Perform:

1. Sit in Dandasana.
2. Bend the left knee and place the sole of the left foot against the right inner thigh, close to the perineum.
3. Inhale, lengthen the spine, raise the hands overhead, exhale, draw the navel in, and start to fold forward, maintaining the length in the spine. Gently grasp the right foot with both hands.
4. Bend the trunk forward with further exhalation and reach the head to the right knee.
5. Stay and breathe here for 30 seconds to 1 minute.
6. Come back to Dandasana and repeat on the other side.

Joint Actions:

- Mild flexion of the spine moves toward extension.
- Abduction and upward rotation of the scapula.
- Flexion, slight external rotation, and adduction of the glenohumeral joint.
- Flexion, adduction, and internal rotation of the hip at the extended leg.
- Extension of the knee at the extended leg.
- Dorsiflexion of the ankle at the extended leg.
- Flexion, abduction, and external rotation of the hip at the folder leg.
- Flexion of the knee at the folded leg.
- Plantarflexion of the ankle at the folded leg.

- Supination of the foot at the folded leg.
- Extension of the elbow.
- Slight pronation of the forearm.

Main Muscle Actions:

- Stretching of the gluteus, hamstring, and calf muscles of the extended leg.
- Contraction of the quads and abdominal muscles.

Things To Focus On:

- Focus on internally rotating the outstretched leg, engage the hip flexors, and press the sole of the opposite foot against the inner thigh.
- Engage the core muscles by tucking the tailbone in so as to fold forward and keep the spine straight and the neck neutral.

Things To Be Cared For:

- People suffering from asthma, diarrhea, lower back injuries, or lumbar disc herniations should avoid doing this pose.
- People with neck, shoulder, lower back, or knee pain should avoid this pose or practice under the supervision of a therapeutic yoga teacher.
- Women who are pregnant or are in their menstrual cycle should avoid this asana.

Janu Sirshasana Urdhva Mukha Variation 1

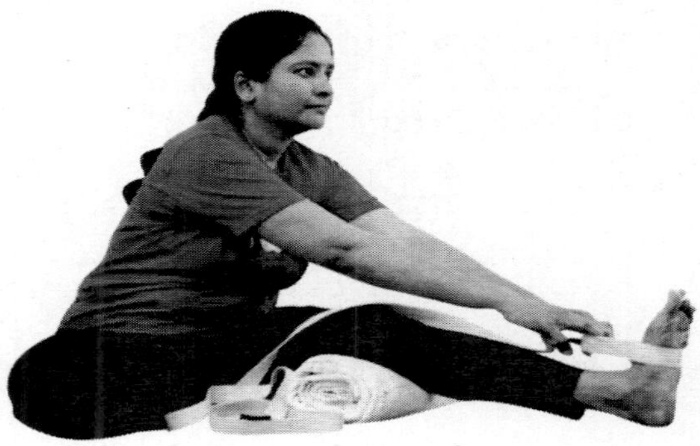

Janu Sirshasana Urdhva Mukha Variation 2

5. Vakrasana (Spinal Twist Pose):

Steps To Perform:

1. Sit in Dandasana.
2. Bend the left knee and place the left foot outside the right knee.
3. Bring the right hand to the outer side of the left leg and try to hold the left foot with the right hand.
4. Inhale, lengthen the spine, exhale, gently twist the torso towards the left, and place the left palm behind the back in between the medians of the buttocks.
5. Stay and breathe here for 30 seconds to 1 minute.
6. Inhale and come back to Dandasana.
7. Interchange the legs and repeat on the other side.

Joint Actions:

- Lateral rotation of the spine.
- Elevation and retraction of the scapula.
- Mild abduction of the shoulder, extension of the elbows, pronation of the forearm, and extension of the wrist.
- Hip in neutral, knee extension, and foot plantar flexion of the extended leg.
- Hip in neutral, knee flexion, and foot in the neutral position of the bent leg.
- Lateral rotation of the cervical spine.

Main Muscle Actions:

- Lateral rotators of spine muscles.
- Flexors of hip muscles and knee flexor muscles of the bent leg.

- Semispinalis cervicis, multifidus scalene muscles, splenius capitis, and sternocleidomastoid muscles of the neck.

Things To Focus On:

- Focus on keeping the sole of the foot on the bent knee completely on the mat by rooting the big toe without lifting the inner edges of the foot.
- Engage hip flexors and core muscles, and then twist. Focus on pulling the navel away from the thigh and hugging the knee, enabling you to create space to breathe while twisting.
- Focus on keeping the spine straight and the shoulders in line in the final position, and do not lean on the arm placed behind the buttocks.

Things To Be Cared For:

- People with neck or shoulder pain should avoid this pose or practice under the supervision of a therapeutic yoga teacher.
- People with headaches, insomnia, exhaustion, or low blood pressure should avoid this asana.
- Women who are pregnant or are in their menstrual cycle should avoid this asana.

Vakrasana Variation 1

Vakrasana Variation 2

6. Supta Virasana (Reclined Hero Pose):

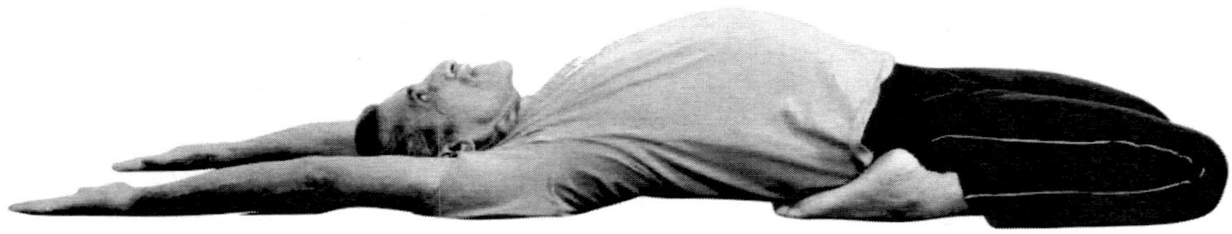

Steps To Perform:

1. Sit in Vajrasana and slide the heels by the sides of the buttocks, bringing the buttocks on the mat in between the heels.
2. Exhale, gently lean back, hold the heels, place the elbows on the floor, and rest the back on the mat.
3. Inhale, raise the arms, extend them overhead, and keep the palms facing upward.
4. Stay and breathe here for 30 seconds to 2 minutes.
5. Come back to Vajrasana.

Joint Actions:

- Lumbar extension of the spine.
- Upward rotation and elevation of the scapula.
- Flexion, external rotation, and glenohumeral joint.
- Anterior pelvic tilt.
- Internal rotation and mild abduction of the hip.
- Flexion of the knee.
- Plantarflexion of the ankle.

Main Muscle Actions:

- Erector spinae muscles.
- Retractors of the shoulder muscles.
- Knee flexor muscles.

Things To Focus On:

- Focus on internally rotating the hips and drawing the knees together since there is a tendency for the hips to rotate externally and the knees to go wider while leaning back.
- Engage the muscles of the lower back while leaning backward, and gently rest the upper back and head on the mat.

Things To Be Cared For:

- Do not practice it with partially blocked arteries or those who have undergone bypass surgery recently.
- Avoid practicing this pose if you are suffering from issues with the back, knee, or ankle. However, with the doctor's advice to practice yoga, one can practice under the supervision of a therapeutic yoga teacher.

Supta Veerasana Variation 1

Supta Veerasana Variation 2

7. Pashu Vishram Asana (Relaxing Animal Pose):

Steps To Perform:

1. Sit in Dandasana, bend the left knee, and place the left heel against the right thigh close to the perineum.
2. Bend the right knee and place the right heel by the side of the right buttock.
3. Inhale, lengthen the spine, extend the arms over the head, exhale, fold forward, and bring the forehead down on the mat with the arms extended in front of the head.
4. Stay and breathe here for 30 seconds to 2 minutes.
5. Come up and repeat on the other side by interchanging the legs.

Joint Actions:

- Forward flexion of the spine.
- Flexion of the shoulder and elevation and retraction of the scapula.
- Extension of the elbow.
- Pronation of the forearm.
- Hip adduction, flexion, and external rotation on one side.
- Hip adduction, flexion, and internal rotation on the other side.
- Knee flexion and ankle plantar flexion.

Main Muscle Actions:

- Stretching of the erector spinae muscles.
- Hip flexors and knee flexor muscles.

Things To Focus On:

- Focus on placing the heel of the foot closer to the navel by drawing the navel in, engaging the core muscles while folding forward.
- Keep the neck neutral without turning it sideways.

Things To Be Cared For:

- People who have serious lower back injuries, hypertension, or hip injuries should practice under the supervision of a therapeutic yoga teacher.

Pashu Vishramasana Variation 1

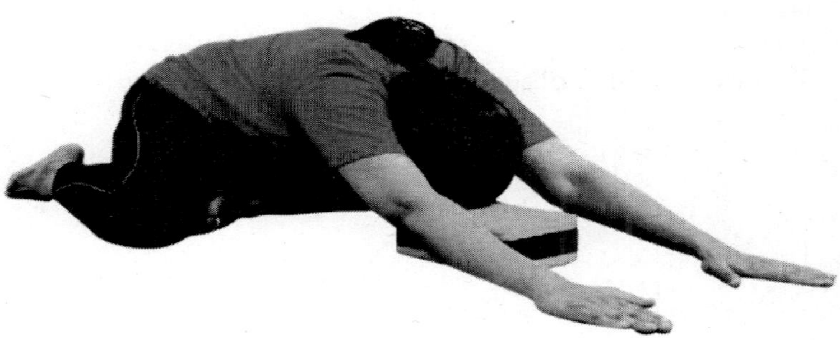

Pashu Vishramasana Variation Side View

8. Supta Baddakon Asana (Reclined Bound Angle Pose):

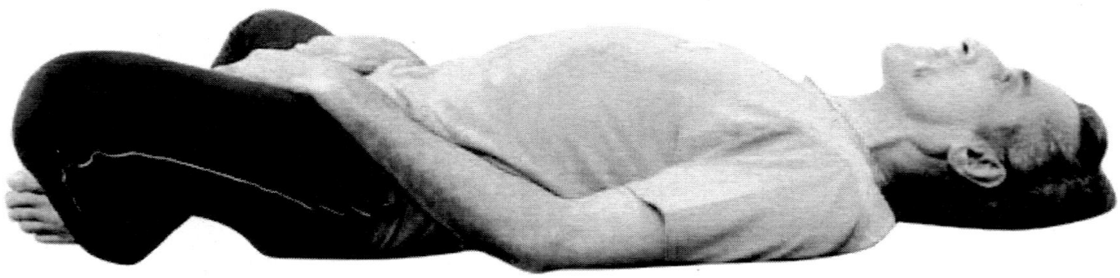

Steps To Perform:

1. Sit in Sukhasana.
2. Gently join the soles of the feet together and draw the heels close to the perineum.
3. Inhale, lengthen the spine, exhale, gently place the elbows by the sides of the buttocks, and rest the back and head on the mat.
4. Place the palms on the thighs.
5. Stay here and breathe for 30 seconds to 2 minutes.
6. Come up with an inhalation.

Joint Actions:

- Lumbar and thoracic extensions.
- Slight abduction of shoulder and elbow flexion.
- External rotation, flexion, and abduction of the hip.
- Flexion of the knees.
- Inversion of the foot.
- Pronation of the forearms.

Main Muscle Actions:

- Erector spinae muscles.
- Shoulder retractors muscles.
- Stretching of hip adductors.
- Hip and knee flexors are group muscles.

Things To Focus On:

- Focus on externally rotating the hips by engaging the hip flexors and adductor muscles of the thighs to push the knees sideways as close as possible towards the ground.

- Engage the lower back muscles when lengthening the spine and resting backward.

Things To Be Cared For:

- People suffering from injuries to the knees, groin, and hips are not supposed to practice this asana.

- Although this pose does bring relief to the nerve, in severe cases of sciatica, it may cause discomfort. Hence, it is better to avoid this pose.

- Women who are pregnant and people suffering from lower back pain should practice under the supervision of a therapeutic yoga teacher.

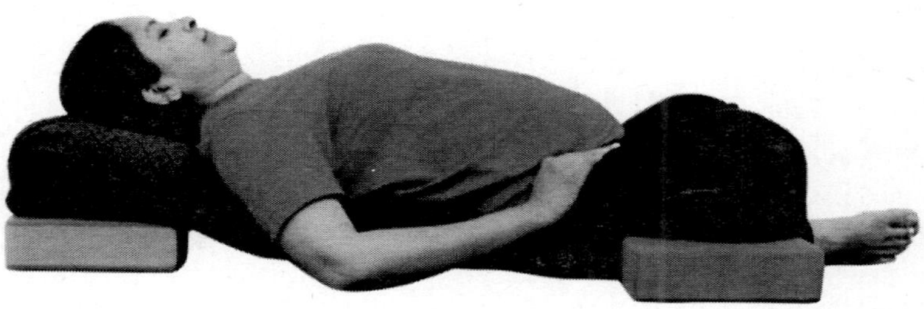

Supta Baddakonasana Variation 1

Supta Baddakonasana Variation 2

9. Makarasana (Crocodile Pose):

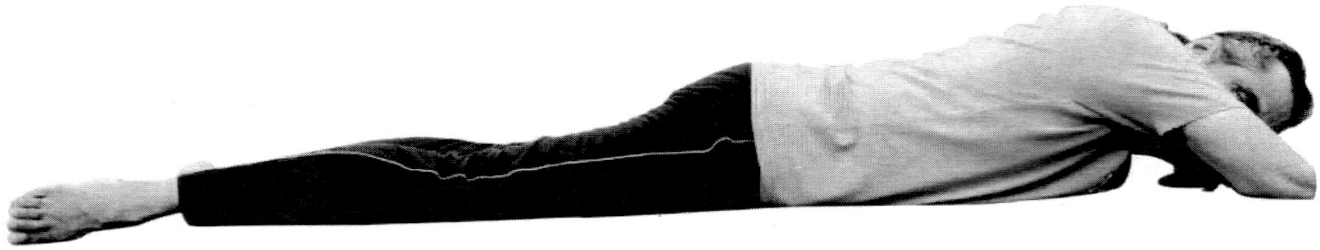

Steps To Perform:

1. Lie on the belly, with the legs spread mat width apart, toes pointing out, bend the elbows, point them sideways, and rest one palm on top of the other.

2. Rest the cheek on the palms.

3. Stay and breathe here for 30 seconds to 5 minutes.

Joint Actions:

- Neutral position of the spine.
- Retraction of the scapula.
- Flexion of the bilateral elbow, shoulders, 90-degree abduction.
- Abduction and internal rotation of the hip.
- Extension of the knee.
- Eversion of ankles.

Main Muscle Actions:

- Erector spinae muscles.
- Middle fibers of deltoid muscles.

Things To Focus On:

- Focus on normal inhalation and exhalation without forcing the breath in any way that relaxes the entire body.

Things To Be Cared For:

- People with back and neck injuries and deep psychological issues should practice this asana only under the supervision of a therapeutic yoga teacher.

10. Shavasana (Corpse Pose):

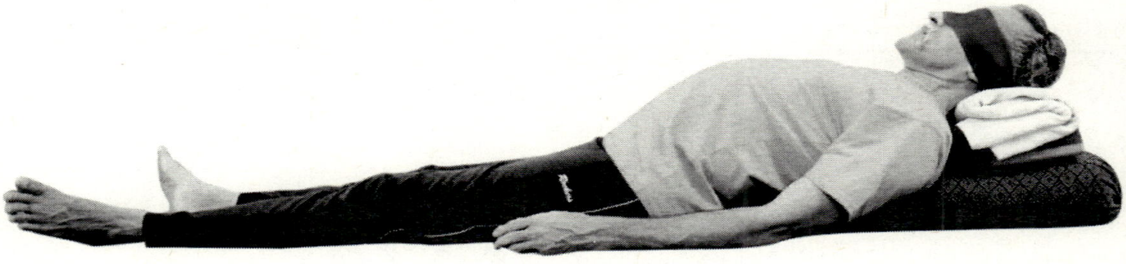

Steps To Perform:

1. Lie down on the back, spreading the legs mat width apart, arms slightly away from the body, palms facing upwards, and fingers naturally curled.

2. Close the eyes and relax the entire body from head to toe, bringing awareness to every part of the body.

3. Stay and breathe normally for 5 to 10 minutes.

Things To Focus On:

- Focus on staying still and relaxing the entire body without moving any part of the body or contracting any muscles.

- Focus on keeping the eyes closed and just observe the natural flow of breath without falling asleep.

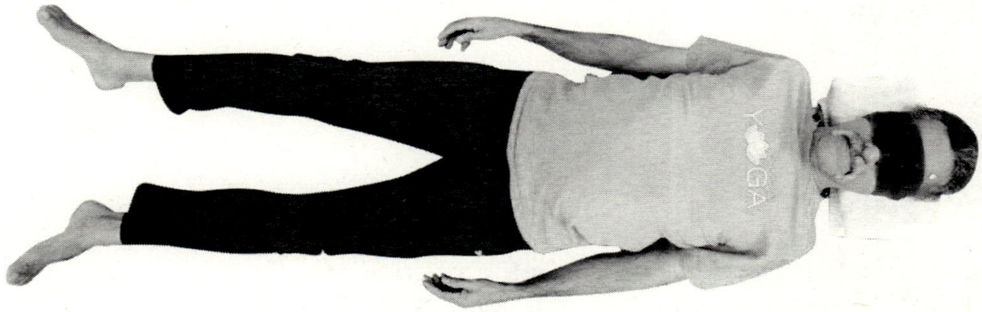

Treatment for Stress:

Ayurveda:

- Lifestyle modifications.
- Head massage with oil.
- Physical exercise (Vyayam).
- Satwavajaya Chikitsa (Psychotherapy).
- Panchakarma (Snehanas, Nasyas, and Shishodhara).
- Rasayana Chikitsa (Rejuvenation Therapies).
- Herbs like Ashwagandha, Brahmi, Jyotishmati, and Jatamansi help in blood circulation towards the brain and release stress.
- Therapies like Shirodara, Shirobasti, Abhyanga Natailadhara, and Ksheeradhara.

Allopathy:

- Regular medications.

Pranayama:

- Abdominal Breathing.
- Viloma Pranayama (3 Levels).
- Jal Neti (since it balances the left and right hemispheres of the brain).
- Ujjayi Pranayama.
- Nadi Shodhana.
- Moorcha Pranayama.

Nutrition for Stress:

Stress eating or emotional eating is a common practice of indulging in comfort food as a way to suppress negative emotions, which may lead to overeating. This, in turn, may become a habit, causing obesity, diabetes, heart issues, and other ailments.

When one is stressed, the adrenal glands secrete cortisol and epinephrine, which are stress hormones, into the bloodstream. They cause an increase in heart rate and blood pressure, which is a natural fight or flight response to certain situations.

Therefore, most often, people undergoing stress end up making the wrong choices in food and munching on high-calorie, fatty foods.

When it comes to making a healthy choice in food, it's best to consume foods that help increase the level of serotonin, a calming hormone, to reduce stress hormones.

Foods to Consume:

Foods Rich in Vitamin C	Oranges, kiwis, guava, lychees, papaya, strawberries, lemon, broccoli, tomatoes, kale, parsley
Foods Rich in Iron & Magnesium	Avocados, sweet potatoes, green leafy vegetables
Nuts & Seeds	Almonds, cashews, walnuts, peanuts, pistachios, pumpkin seeds, flax seeds
Legumes	Chickpeas, rajma, soybean
Whole Grains	Barley, wheat, ragi, buckwheat, quinoa
Vegetables	Cucumber, carrots, radish, beetroot, okra, mushrooms
Others	Skim or low-fat milk when had before bed can help ease stress and anxiety; Chamomile tea can help reduce stress and help promote sleep

Foods to Avoid:

- Spicy foods: chilies, jalapenos, peppers, onions, and ginger.
- Refined carbohydrates.
- Fried/oily food.
- Foods and drinks high in sugar.
- Caffeine: coffee, tea, and energy drinks.
- Non-vegetarian food: red meat.
- Smoking and alcohol.

It is advisable to have 40 to 60 minutes of daily physical activity like walking, jogging, yoga, etc. Along with pranayama and meditation, it plays an important part in keeping stress and anxiety at bay.

THYROID

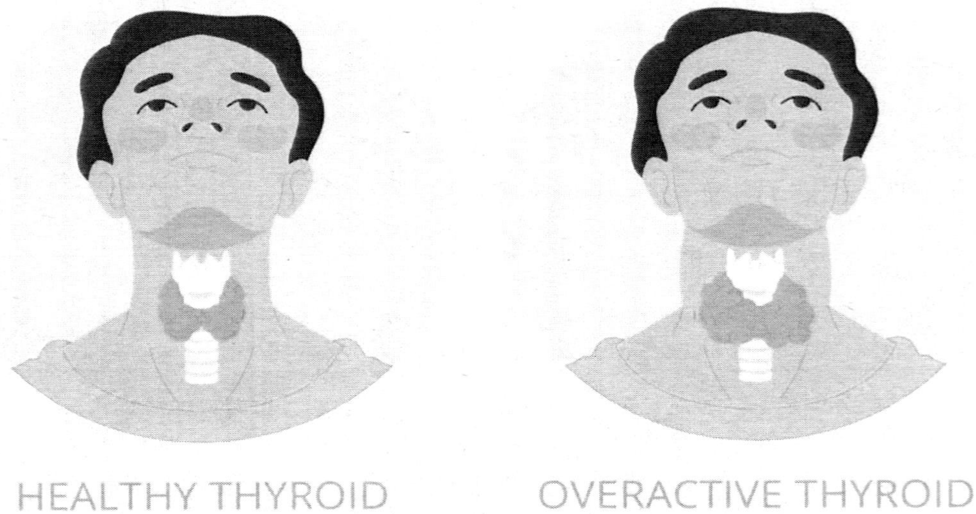

The thyroid is a small, butterfly-shaped gland in our body, located above the windpipe in the neck, just below the larynx, with two connected lobes on either side of the trachea. It produces thyroxine/tetraiodothyronine (T4) and triiodothyronine (T3).

The secretion of thyroid hormones T3 and T4 plays a vital role in metabolic, cardiovascular, and developmental factors in our body. It also plays a role in maintaining sleep, sexual function, and thoughts. Thyroid disorder can affect almost all organs, including the heart.

Thyroid disorders can be classified mainly into two types:

- **Hyperthyroidism:** It is a condition where there is an excessive generation of thyroid hormones.
- **Hypothyroidism:** It is a condition where there is insufficient production of thyroid hormones.

Some other types of thyroid disorders include:

- **Goiter:** A condition where the thyroid gland is enlarged.
- **Thyroid Nodules:** A condition in which there are lumps in the thyroid gland.
- **Thyroiditis:** A condition in which there is inflammation of the thyroid gland.
- **Thyroid Cancer.**

Although classical Ayurvedic texts do not explicitly mention diseases like hypothyroidism or hyperthyroidism, a condition called Galaganda, or neck swelling, is a common symptom in both. Charaka Samhita mentions a condition under Shleshma Vikara. Acharya Sushruta also clearly mentions the basis of Galaganda; out of seven layers of the skin, the 6th layer, known as Rohini, is the site for the establishment of the disease Galaganda, which is closely associated with goiter (abnormal swelling of the thyroid gland).

As a symptom of thyroid disease, goiter is generally associated with hyperthyroidism but can also occur with hypothyroidism. Thus, it is possibly insignificant to draw a correlation between hypothyroidism and Galaganda. Also, while there is no direct mention of the thyroid gland and hyperthyroidism in Ayurveda, there are similarities in the pathogenesis of Bhasmak Rog (insatiable appetite) and hyperthyroidism, and hence, they are sometimes correlated. It can be caused by atyagni (excessive digestion) or tikshnagni (quick digestion) due to Pitta Vriddhi. In the 16th century, there is mention of Bhasmaka Roga in Madhyam Khanda as Jathragni Vikara (digestive fire).

According to Ayurveda, hypothyroidism is caused by an imbalance in the Vata or Kapha dosha, and hyperthyroidism is due to an imbalance in the Pitta dosha. At times, it can happen in a more complex presentation. The symptoms of hypothyroidism depend on the type of dosha imbalance:

- If Kapha dosha is dominant and aggravating, one may experience symptoms like malaise, lethargy, slow speech, slow pulse, poor appetite, weight gain, thick skin, goiter, and puffy eyes.
- If Vata dosha is dominant, one may experience symptoms like fatigue, constipation, muscle cramps, dry skin, weakness, and diminution in the dhatu.

Causes:

The under- or over functioning of the thyroid gland can be due to iodine deficiency, autoimmune diseases, inflammation in the thyroid gland (thyroiditis), a non-functioning thyroid gland, or nodules that are overactive inside the thyroid gland, which can cause toxic multinodular goiter.

Symptoms:

The symptoms can vary depending on the type of thyroid disease in a person. Some of the common symptoms are:

Thyroid Nodules:

(There can be no symptoms found under this condition.)

Hyperthyroidism:

- Weight loss for no apparent reason.

- Irregular or rapid heartbeat.
- Sweating, anxiety, and nervousness.
- Muscle weakness.
- Abnormal or skipped menstrual cycle.
- Diarrhea.

Hypothyroidism:

- Intolerance to cold temperatures.
- Weight gain.
- Fatigue (tiredness).
- Mental dullness (brain fog) and depression.
- Frequent and heavy menstrual periods with mood swings.
- Hair loss, hoarse voice, weak nails.
- Sensitivity to cold and dry skin.
- Constipation.

Diagnosis:

- **Physical Exams:** Palpitation of the neck for any growths or enlargements of the thyroid.
- **Laboratory Tests:**
    - T4 Test: A blood test is done to measure the thyroid hormone (thyroxine).
    - T3 Total Test: This test is used to measure the thyroid hormone (triiodothyronine).
    - TSH Test: This thyroid-stimulating hormone (TSH) test is done to determine the functioning of the thyroid gland.
    - Thyroid Antibody Test: This test is done to measure the levels of thyroid antibodies in the blood.
    - Imaging Tests: This test is used to find out the cause of thyroid disease.
    - Ultrasound: This test is used to closely look at the thyroid nodules for any tumor growth, cysts, or goiters.

Yogic Intervention:

Regular practice of yoga is an effective way to manage the symptoms of hypo- or hyperthyroidism. Studies have shown that poses that stimulate the thyroid gland help balance endocrine hormones. Also, since stress is one of the main reasons for developing thyroid issues, practicing yoga regularly reduces stress and anxiety drastically.

Case Study:

Subjective: A schoolgirl, Madhavi (name changed), aged 14 years, studying in 9th grade, had issues of weight gain and mood swings.

Objective: After consultation with an endocrinologist, she was diagnosed with hypothyroidism.

Assessment: Doctors prescribed medications for thyroid and advised her to start a fitness regimen to maintain her weight. Although Madhavi was taking medication as prescribed and had joined a weight loss program at a gym, she didn't feel much of a change. Her mother did some research, following which she reached out to us to inquire about yoga for her daughter's problem.

Plan: We suggested her mother enroll her in our regular yoga session for a few months until she could manage to do the movements in yoga, after which we advised her to start with yoga therapy sessions. She is now 24 years old and pursuing her master's in business administration. She has been practicing yoga ever since, which is helping her manage her weight and mood swings immensely.

- **Surya Namaskar (Sun Salutations):**

Regular practice of Surya Namaskars can be beneficial.

- **Asanas (Yoga Postures):**

The following are some postures that are helpful in managing thyroid:

1. Marjari-Bitilasana (Cat Cow Pose):

Bitilasana Main Pose

Marjariasana Main Pose

Steps To Perform:

1. Come up on the knees and hands, with the back forming a tabletop.
2. Stack the shoulders on top of the wrist with the palms shoulder-width apart and the knees trunk-width apart.
3. Inhale, arch the back, raise the chin, and gently tilt the head back.
4. Exhale, rounding the back, bringing the chin to the chest.
5. Repeat this movement 10 times.
6. Come back to the neutral position.

Joint Actions:

- Extension of the spine with retraction of the scapula when the back is arched.
- Flexion of the spine with protraction of the scapula when the back is rounded.
- Flexion and adduction of the shoulders, elbow extension, and wrist extension.
- Flexion of the hip and knee with plantar flexion of the ankles.

Main Muscle Actions:

- Cat pose muscle action is stretching of the erector spinae, gluteal muscles, and levator scapulae muscles.
- Cow pose muscle action is a contraction of the erector spinae and trapezius muscles.

Things To Focus On:

- Focus on engaging the core by drawing the navel in as you arch and round the back.
- Engage the tips of the fingers, balls, and heels of the palms and push the chest and shoulders away from the floor as you round the back.
- Keep a stable base without moving the palms or knees when in the pose.

Things To Be Cared For:

- People with severe back, neck, knee, or head injuries should avoid practicing this pose.
- Pregnant women should practice this pose under the supervision of a therapeutic yoga teacher.

2. Ardha Ushtrasana (Half Camel Pose):

It is a good posture for developing flexibility in the spine and neck.

Steps To Perform:

1. Come on the knees, keeping them hip-width apart.
2. Roll the shoulders back and place the palms on the buttocks, moving the elbows close to each other.
3. Inhale, lengthen the torso, and arch the back.
4. Exhale and slowly drop the head back.
5. Stay and breathe here for 30 seconds to 1 minute.
6. Inhale and come back to the starting position.

Joint Actions:

- Extension of the spine.
- Extension of the shoulder with retraction of the scapula.
- Slight flexion of the elbow, pronation of the forearm, and wrist extension.
- Slight extension of the hip with flexion of the knee and plantar flexion of the ankle.

Main Muscle Actions:

- Contraction of the erector spinae and gluteal muscles.
- Stretching of hip flexor muscles and rectus and transversus abdominis muscles.

Things To Focus On:

- Focus on lifting the sternum to raise the chest.
- Squeeze the buttocks to activate the glutes.
- Focus on rolling the shoulders back and down to push the chest up towards the ceiling by engaging the upper back.
- Do not pinch the shoulders together, causing tension in the neck.
- Do not crunch the lower back by squeezing the glutes too much or pushing the knees wider than hip-width apart.

Things To Be Cared For:

- Avoid this pose if you suffer from insomnia, serious neck problems, or injuries to the abdomen, back, and knees.
- People suffering from migraine, high blood pressure, and vertigo should practice this pose under the supervision of a therapeutic yoga teacher.

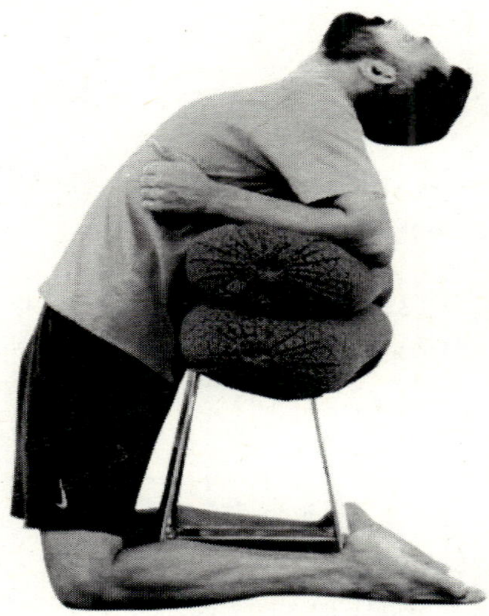

Ardha Ushtrasana
Variation 1

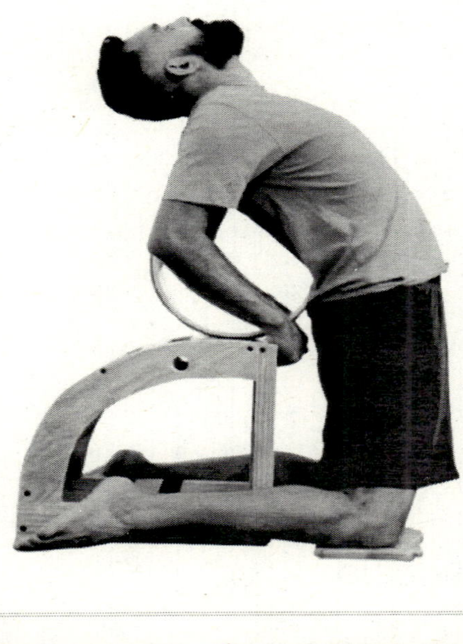

Ardha Ushtrasana
Variation 2

3. Dhanurasana (Bow Pose):

Steps To Perform:

1. Lie on the belly.
2. Bend the knees and grab hold of the ankles on either side with the hands.
3. Inhale, lift the head and chest up, arching the back; exhale, lift the thighs, and push the ankles away from the hands.
4. Stay here and breathe for 30 seconds to 1 minute.
5. Exhale and release.

Joint Actions:

- Extension of the spine.
- Extension of the shoulder with extension of the elbow, mid-prone position of the elbow.
- Extension of the hip with flexion of the knees and ankle in plantar flexion.

Main Muscle Actions:

- Contraction of the erector spinae, gluteal muscles, and hamstring muscles.
- Stretching of the rectus and transversus abdominis muscles and the hip flexor muscle group.

Things To Focus On:

- Focus on rolling the shoulders back and squeezing the shoulder blades close to each other to expand the chest, creating space to breathe as you push the chest away from the floor.

- Focus on keeping the lower limbs active, from the glutes to the toes.
- Keep the neck neutral.

Things To Be Cared For:

- People with lower back pain, neck pain, or joint pain should practice this pose under the supervision of a therapeutic yoga teacher.
- Pregnant women, women in the menstrual cycle, people with high or low BP, severe spondylitis, back neck injuries, ulcers, hernias, and recent abdominal surgeries should avoid practicing this pose.

Dhanurasana Variation 1

4. Bhujangasana (Cobra Pose):

Steps To Perform:

1. Lie on the belly, feet hip-width apart, toes pointing back. Place the palms right below the shoulders by the sides of the chest.
2. Inhale, press the palms, and push the chest away from the floor, arching the back without shrugging the shoulders.
3. Stay here and breathe for 30 seconds to 1 minute.
4. Exhale and release.

Joint Actions:

- Extension of the spine.
- Extension of the hip with mild flexion of the knee and plantar flexion of the ankle.
- Mild flexion of the shoulder with extension of elbows and wrist extension.

Main Muscle Actions:

- Contraction of the erector spinae muscles and gluteal muscle group.
- Stretching of the iliacus, quadriceps femoris, rectus, and transversus abdominis muscles.

Things To Focus On:

- Focus on squeezing the glutes and pushing them down, pressing the thighs and toes firmly on the mat to engage the lower limbs.
- Draw the navel in and engage the core to feel the stretch in the abdomen.
- Engage the shoulder blades by rolling them back and down and trying to bring the scapula closer to each other, pushing the chest forward to expand the ribs and create

space to breathe.

- Keep the neck neutral.

Things To Be Cared For:

- People suffering from a hernia or recent back, shoulder, wrist, or hip injury, headaches, or who have undergone recent abdominal surgeries should not practice this pose.
- People with lower back, neck, knee, ankle, and shoulder pain should practice this under the supervision of a therapeutic yoga teacher.
- Women should not practice this pose during pregnancy or the menstrual cycle.

Bhujangasana Variation 1

Bhujangasana Variation 2

5. **Urdhva Mukha Shvanasana (Upward-Facing Dog):**

Steps To Perform:

1. Lie on the belly, feet hip-width apart, toes pointing back, and place the palms right below the shoulders by the sides of the chest.
2. Inhale, press the palms, and push the chest away from the floor, arching the back. Keep the knees and thighs off the floor.
3. Stay here and breathe for 30 seconds to 1 minute.
4. Exhale and release.

Joint Actions:

- Extension of the spine.
- Extension of the hip with mild flexion of the knee and plantar flexion of the ankle.
- Mild flexion of the shoulder with extension of elbows and wrist extension.

Main Muscle Actions:

- Contraction of the erector spinae muscles and gluteal muscle group.
- Stretching of the iliacus, quadriceps femoris, rectus, and transversus abdominis muscles.

Things To Focus On:

- Activate the glutes, quads, and toes to engage the lower limbs. Focus on keeping the knees and thighs off the floor as you arch the back and look up towards the ceiling.
- Draw the navel in and engage the core to feel the stretch in the abdomen.

- Engage the shoulder blades by rolling them back and down and trying to bring the scapula closer to each other, pushing the chest forward to expand the ribs and create space to breathe.
- Keep the neck neutral.

Things To Be Cared For:

- People suffering from a hernia, back injuries, headaches, or who have undergone recent abdominal surgeries, pregnant women, or women in the menstrual cycle should avoid practicing this pose.
- People with lower back, neck, knee, ankle, and shoulder pain should practice this under the supervision of a therapeutic yoga teacher.

Urdhva Mukha Shvanasana Variation 1

Urdhva Mukha Shvanasana Variation 2

6. Ardha Navasana (Half Boat Pose):

Steps To Perform:

1. Sit in Dandasana.
2. Bend the knees, keeping the feet on the mat and hands on the side.
3. Roll the shoulders back and lean slightly on the back.
4. Interlock the fingers at the back of the head.
5. Inhale, lift the feet off the floor, and extend the legs, keeping the toes in line with the forehead. Balance on the sitz bone.
6. Stay here and breathe for 30 seconds to 1 minute.
7. Exhale and lower the legs; release the hands, coming to Dandasana.

Joint Actions:

- Flexion of the lumbar spine.
- Abduction with flexion of the shoulder, flexion of the elbow, and forearm pronation.
- Flexion of the hip with extended knees and ankle in plantar flexion.

Main Muscle Actions:

- Contraction of the rectus and transversus abdominis muscles, the hip flexor muscle group, and the quadriceps femoris and gastrocnemius muscles.
- Stretching of the levator scapulae and gluteal muscles.

Things To Focus On:

- Focus on engaging the abdominal muscles by drawing the navel in. Keep the shoulders rolled back, pushing the chest forward, expanding the rib cage, and creating space to breathe without rounding the back.

- Activate the quads by squeezing the thighs close to each other.
- Keep the neck neutral.

Things To Be Cared For:

- People suffering from asthma, diarrhea, insomnia, heavy-headedness, or injuries on the neck, back, hip, knee, or ankle should avoid practicing this pose.
- People with lower back pain or tailbone issues should practice this under the supervision of a therapeutic yoga teacher.
- Women should avoid practicing this pose during pregnancy and the menstrual cycle.

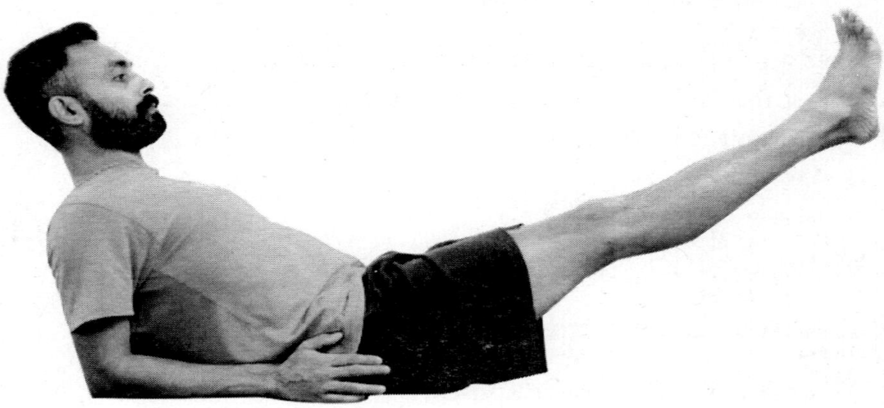

Ardha Navasana Variation 1

Ardha Navasana Variation 2

7. **Salamba Sarvangasana (Supported Shoulder Stand):**

Steps To Perform:

1. Lie down on the back with the feet stretched forward, feet together, and palms by the sides of the body.
2. Bend the knees, bring them towards the chest, and place the palms on the sides of the hips.
3. Inhale, lift the legs and hips up, and support the back with the palms. Keep lifting the trunk and straightening the legs in line with the hips and the shoulders.
4. Stay and breathe here for 30 seconds to 1 minute.
5. Bend the knees and bring the thighs close to the belly; gently roll the spine back vertebrae by vertebrae; and come back to the neutral position.

Joint Actions:

- Retraction of the scapula.
- Extension, abduction, and external rotation of the shoulder.
- Flexion of the cervical and thoracic spines.
- Flexion of the elbow with supination of the forearm.
- Neutral position of the hip with knee extension and plantar flexion of the ankle.

Main Muscle Actions:

- Contraction of gluteal muscles and quadricep muscles.
- It stretches the cervical extensor muscle group.
- Contraction of the biceps and supinator muscles.

Things To Focus On:

- Keep your core engaged by drawing your navel in as you lift the legs, and do not allow the belly to pop up.
- Keep the neck relaxed and neutral, and rest the palms firmly on the back as you lift the leg for support.

Things To Be Cared For:

- People suffering from a throat or ear infection, migraine, severe back pain or spine injury, ulcer, or who have undergone recent abdominal surgery should avoid this asana.
- People suffering from high blood pressure or slipped discs should practice this pose under the supervision of a therapeutic yoga teacher.
- Women should avoid practicing this pose during pregnancy or the menstrual cycle.

Salamba Sarvangasana Variation 1

Salamba Sarvangasana Variation 2

8. Ardha Halasana (Half Plough Pose):

Steps To Perform:

1. Lie on the back with the arms next to the body and the palms on the floor.
2. Inhale, kick up, and lift the legs to 90 degrees. Slowly roll the pelvis off the floor, supporting the hips with palms. Come to the shoulder stand.
3. Exhale, slowly start moving the legs back towards the head, bringing the heels in line with the pelvis, the chin close to the chest, and try to straighten the arms on the mat.
4. Stay and breathe here for 30 seconds to 1 minute.
5. Inhale, come back to the shoulder stand, then slowly roll the spine down on the mat vertebrae by vertebrae, coming back to the starting position.

Joint Actions:

- Flexion of the spine.
- Flexion of the hip with an extended knee and ankle in plantar flexion.
- Extension of elbows with pronation of the forearm.

Main Muscle Actions:

- Contraction of the hip flexor muscle group.
- Contraction of the rectus and transversus abdominis muscles and quadriceps muscles.
- Stretching of the thoracolumbar fascia and gluteal muscles.

Things To Focus On:

- Activate the quads by squeezing the thighs closer.

- Focus on engaging the core muscles and keep the hips off the floor such that the weight is on the shoulders and the upper arms, not the neck.
- Tuck the chin to the chest, keeping the neck relaxed, and gaze towards the navel.

Things To Be Cared For:

- People suffering from back or neck injuries should practice this pose under the supervision of a therapeutic yoga teacher.
- Avoid this pose if you are suffering from diarrhea, and women should avoid this pose during pregnancy and the menstrual cycle.

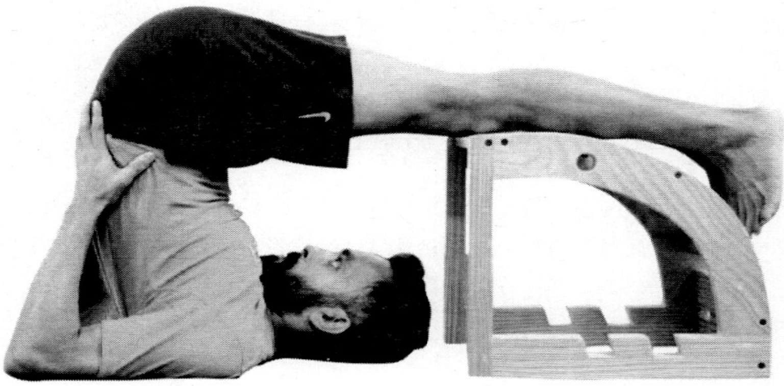

Ardha Halasana Variation 1

Ardha Halasana Variation 2

9. Halasana (Plough Pose):

Steps To Perform:

1. Lie on your back with your arms next to your body and your palms on the floor.
2. Inhale, kick up and lift the legs to 90 degrees, and slowly roll your pelvis off the floor, supporting the hips with the palms, coming to the shoulder stand.
3. Exhale and slowly start moving the legs back towards the head, reaching the toes onto the floor.
4. Stay and breathe here for 30 seconds to 1 minute.
5. Inhale, come back to the shoulder stand, then slowly roll the spine down on the mat vertebrae by vertebrae, coming back to the starting position.

Joint Actions:

- Flexion of the spine.
- Flexion of the hip with knee extensions and the ankle in a neutral position.
- Adduction of the shoulder with elbow extension and the mid-prone position of the forearm.

Main Muscle Actions:

- Contraction of rectus and transversus abdominis muscles, iliacus muscle, quadricep muscles, and shoulder retractors muscle group.
- Stretching of gluteus muscles and thoracolumbar fascia.

Things To Focus On:

- Activate the quads by squeezing the thighs closer.

- Focus on engaging the core muscles and keeping the hips lifted such that the weight is on the shoulders and the upper arms, not the neck.
- Tuck the chin to the chest, keeping the neck relaxed, and gaze towards the navel.

Things To Be Cared For:

- People suffering from back or neck injuries should practice this pose under the supervision of a therapeutic yoga teacher.
- Avoid this pose if you are suffering from diarrhea, and women should avoid this pose during pregnancy and the menstrual cycle.

Halasana Variation 1

Halasana Variation 2

Treatment for Stress:

Treatment for thyroid can be done in a variety of ways, and each treatment depends on the cause of the thyroid condition.

Ayurveda:

Treatment is based on the severity of the condition, and it's best to consult an Ayurvedic doctor for the same. Some of the common treatments could include:

- Snehapana (Oleation).
- Samshodana Chikitsa (Cleaning).
- Vamana (Medically induced vomiting).
- Mridu Virechana (Therapeutic Purgation).
- Samsamana Chikitsa (Palliative Care).
- Nasya (Nasal Treatment).
- Shirodhara.
- Siraa Vyadhana (Venesection) in the management of excess rakta in quantity.

Along with standard treatments, Ayurvedic medicine can be used to help manage thyroid disorders. Many Ayurvedic herbs are used, including Trikatu, Triphala, Jatamansi, Shilajit, Shankhpushpi, and Brahmi, depending on body type and condition. Also, diet and exercise play a very important role in managing symptoms of the thyroid, as per Ayurveda.

Allopathy:

Treatment for thyroid disease varies depending on the nature of the disorder in the thyroid gland. However, the treatment may consist of observation, medication, surgery, or a radioactive iodine uptake test.

Many thyroid nodules show no symptoms, but even if the nodules are detected, they can be treated even without surgery.

For hypothyroidism, consumption of pills on a regular basis is advised. Regular blood tests must be done to check the thyroid hormone levels, which can be helpful for the doctor to adjust the dosage levels.

For hyperthyroidism, medicines that prevent the thyroid gland from secreting high levels of hormones are advised.

- **Beta-Blockers:** Medicines that can reduce symptoms of hyperthyroidism, such as tremors, heart palpitations, and heart rate.

- **Radioiodine Therapy:** This treatment is usually done for hyperthyroidism and for certain types of thyroid cancer, which are targeted to the thyroid cells.
- **Thyroidectomy:** It involves surgically removing the entire or a part of the thyroid gland.

Pranayama:

- Abdominal breathing.
- Viloma pranayama (3 levels).
- Bhastrika or Kapalabhati.
- Bhramari pranayama (the position of the neck should be according to hypo and hyper thyroid).
- Surya bheda pranayama, Swana pranayama (hypothyroidism).

Nutrition for Thyroid:

Thyroid imbalances, which may lead to hyperthyroidism, hypothyroidism, goiter, etc., have a negative effect on the body's metabolism and secretion of hormones. This may lead to weight gain, weight loss, irregular periods in women, anxiety, depression, etc.

Hormones released by the thyroid gland are triiodothyronine (T3) and thyroxine (T4), which help in weight regulation, balance of energy levels, metabolism, etc. Undersecretion or oversecretion of these hormones can lead to thyroid imbalances.

Certain lifestyle changes, like following a healthy diet, avoiding foods that may trigger the thyroid gland, and regular practice of yoga and pranayama, can help balance the hormones.

Dietary Recommendations for Hypothyroidism:

Foods To Consume:

1. **Iodine:** The thyroid gland is the only gland that stores iodine in the body. Iodine deficiency is one of the main reasons for hypothyroidism and goiter. Some iodine-rich sources include.

Plant Based	Iodized salt, seaweed, kelp, whole grain bread, cereals, prunes (dried plums); Other good sources include plants grown in iodine rich soil
Animal Based	Eggs, shrimp, fish - tuna, cod; Seafood is naturally rich in iodine.

2. **Selenium:** Selenium is an integral part of selenoprotein, a critical enzyme in thyroid hormone synthesis. Selenium deficiency exacerbates iodine deficiency and, in combination, contributes to hypothyroidism. Some selenium-rich sources include.

Plant Based	Brazil nuts (one of the highest sources of selenium), cashews, whole wheat bread, whole grain cereals, brown rice, mushrooms, spinach, lentils
Animal Based	Seafood - bangda fish, crab, shrimp, oyster, sardines, salmon; Chicken, turkey, eggs

3. **Iron:** Iron deficiency also impairs the synthesis of thyroid hormones. Some iron-rich sources include.

Plant Based	Pumpkin seeds, legumes - chickpeas, soybean, rajma, flax seeds, nuts - almonds, cashews, dried fruits - apricots, raisins, prunes, whole grains - wheat, brown rice, oats, spinach, iron fortified cereals and bread
Animal Based	Red meat - highest source of iron, eggs, shellfish

Foods to Avoid/ Lower in Consumption:

Goitrogens are substances found in certain plant foods that disrupt the production of thyroid hormones by interfering with iodine uptake in the thyroid gland. There are two main categories of goitrogens:

1. **Cruciferous Vegetables:** Cauliflower, cabbage, broccoli, radish, horseradish, turnips, bamboo shoots, cassava.

2. **Soy and Soy Products:** Soy contains isoflavones that interfere with thyroid function. Millets also contain these isoflavones and behave in the same way. The only restriction is that soy and soy products should not be consumed right after consuming oral thyroid medication, as it interferes with the absorption of hormones, making it difficult to correct hypothyroidism.

Other goitrogens include lima beans, sweet potatoes, sorghum, and linseeds. Dairy products, caffeine, alcohol, and smoking are also to be avoided.

Studies have shown that cooking, steaming, and boiling cruciferous vegetables lead to a reduction in the concentration of glucosinolates in broccoli (Source).

There are no studies that tell us how much cruciferous vegetables or soy products are safe to consume. They can be consumed occasionally rather than being cut out completely.

Dietary Recommendations for Hyperthyroidism:

Foods to Consume:

- Low-iodine foods: non-iodized salt, vegetables, pasta, rice, egg whites, bread, and fresh fruits.

Foods to Avoid:

- Fish and seafood, egg yolk, dairy products, alcohol, and smoking.

Several foods mentioned above fall under the tamasic category, like fish, meat, and others, which, when consumed in excess, lead to lethargy, weight gain, etc. It is best to choose foods that are sattvic in nature, like fresh fruits and vegetables; however, moderate consumption of rajasic and tamasic foods is acceptable.

ACIDITY & GASTRITIS

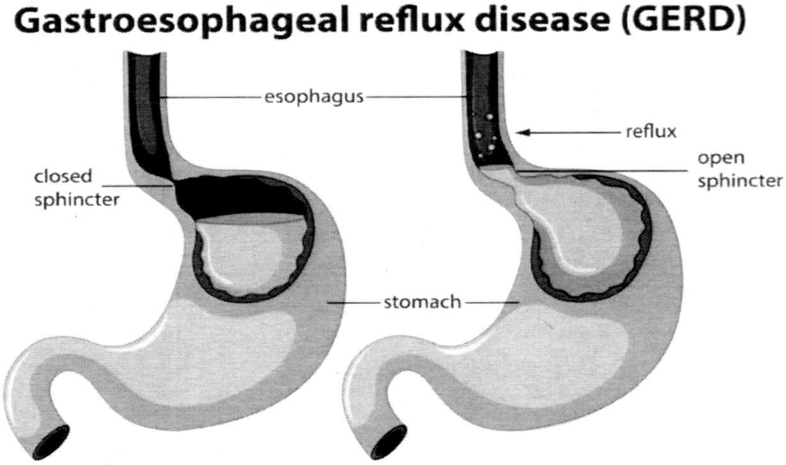

Gastritis is an inflammation, irritation, or erosion of the lining of the stomach due to excess secretion of acids. To digest food, the stomach secretes water, enzymes, gastric juice, acids, etc. Gastric motility and secretion are regulated by neural and humoral mechanisms. Where there is excess secretion of acid, a burning sensation is felt around the lower chest as the gastric juice flows back up into the food pipe (esophagus), commonly called acidity.

A person is diagnosed with GERD (gastroesophageal reflux disease) when acidity is chronic with heartburn. Prolonged acidity might lead to more serious conditions like esophagitis, ulcers, strictures, aspiration pneumonia, etc.

Gas in the stomach, which causes bloating, burping, and flatulence, is called a gastric problem. Although gas is common and natural, when consumed in excess, it can lead to gastroenteritis. People with this condition are highly prone to developing complaints like a bloating sensation, indigestion, stomach cramps, constipation, heartburn, acid reflux, diarrhea, etc.

According to Ayurveda, the condition of hyperacidity is referred to as "Amla Pitta," which comes from two words: "amla" (sour) and "pitta" (gastric, pancreatic, and bile juices). This condition is mentioned in the later Ayurvedic literature of Madhava Nidana. In Amla Pitta, the amount of Pachaka Pitta (gastric juice) increases due to various causes such as constipation and indigestion, and its usual bitter taste (alkaline) changes to a very sour (acidic) taste due to fermentation. Due to this increase in the sour quantity of pitta (stomach juice), it is called amla pitta (hyperacidity). It is a disease of the AnnavahaSrotas (gastrointestinal tract) due to the unusual secretion of enzymes in the stomach and pancreas.

Causes:

Some of the causes of gastritis include:

- Alteration in gut bacteria, constipation.
- Excessive alcohol use and smoking.
- Some non-steroidal anti-inflammatory drugs.
- Eating or drinking too quickly, chewing gum, or drinking from a straw.
- Gastrointestinal infection, blockage, or disease.

Some of the causes of acidity include:

- Excess production of gastric juice, consumption of spicy food, and excessive caffeine intake.
- Stress, indigestion, Helicobacter pylori infection, and food poisoning.
- Unhealthy eating habits, soft drinks and soda, and smoking,
- Stress and lack of sleep.

Symptoms:

People with acidity problems may have at least one or more of the symptoms mentioned below:

- Burning feeling in the stomach, also called heartburn.
- Regurgitation (backwash) of food, bile, or stomach acid, which occurs post-meal or immediately after eating.
- Difficulty swallowing (dysphagia) is due to the excess acid collected in the stomach, causing a feeling of fullness.
- Irritation in the vocal cord is due to the acid moving up to the mouth, leading to a sore throat.
- Indigestion, also known as dyspepsia, can also be a prime sign of acidity.
- Stomach ulcers, blood discharge with stool, piles, or fissures.

Other common symptoms might include:

- Frequent onset of burping or hiccups.
- Difficulty swallowing or the sensation of food being stuck in the throat.
- Regurgitation (prolonged sour taste in the mouth).

- Post-meal heaviness, stiffness in the stomach, restlessness, nausea, vomiting, and sudden loss of weight.
- Discharge of blood with stool and high fever result in stomach ulcers, piles, or fissures.

Diagnosis:

Depending on the symptoms, the doctor may recommend one or more of the following tests for acidity:

- Physical examination.
- Barium swallow.
- Esophageal manometry.
- pH monitoring.
- Endoscopy.
- A biopsy may be taken during endoscopy in more chronic conditions.
- Blood tests, including H. pylori infection.

Again, depending on the symptoms, the doctor may recommend one or more of the following tests for gastritis:

- Personal and family medical history.
- Physical evaluation.
- Upper endoscopy.
- Pernicious anemia and other blood tests.
- Fecal-occult blood test (stool test).

Yogic Intervention:

Research has found that yoga can be a part of treating a person with acidity. Practicing yoga, along with medications, is helpful in combating the symptoms related to digestive disorders. Yoga practice is safe for everyone, restoring our body's natural physiology. It can work wonders for overall health if practiced regularly.

For cervical issues, yoga practice consisting of asanas, pranayama, and certain kriyas has been found to be more beneficial. Asanas that involve twists, turns, and forward bends help squeeze the abdominal organs, thereby releasing gas from the stomach. Certain pranayama practices keep the diaphragm active and healthy, which aids in the digestion process.

Kriyas like kapalabhati, agnisara kriya, and kunjal kriya will also be helpful in cleansing the stomach. Practicing inversions stimulates good venous return and relieves gasses from the large intestines. Lifestyle changes like switching to vegetarian food and reducing the consumption of spicy and junk foods considered harmful to the digestive system are better recommended.

Case Study:

Subjective: A young couple who were IT professionals came with a severe burning sensation in the chest, along with burping and back pain. They had complaints of indigestion as well.

Objective: Upon investigation, the doctor diagnosed them with stress-related acidity and GERD.

Assessment: The doctor prescribed some antacids and tablets to manage the symptoms and suggested they make lifestyle modifications.

Plan: Both of them joined our center after searching on Google for a yoga institution. They were counseled, and then they joined our therapeutic yoga sessions during the weekends. The yoga routine was designed according to their requirements, and some diet modifications had also been advised. After practicing for eight weekends, their condition had improved significantly, and they willingly continued for another eight weekends as they were very happy with their improved health.

Presently, they often come to the yoga center (two to three sessions) for some corrections in their practice and have been managing GERD efficiently.

- **Surya Namaskar (Sun Salutation):**

A modified version of Surya Namaskar, which involves staying for multiple breaths in Pada Hastasana (Forward Fold) and Parvatasana (Mountain Pose), can be practiced.

- **Asanas (Yoga Postures):**

The following are some postures that are helpful in managing acidity and gastrtitis:

1.Pada Hastasana (Hand to Foot Pose):

Steps To Perform:

1. Stand in Tadasana.

2. Inhale, lengthen the spine, stretch the arms above the head, exhale, draw the navel in, and start to bend the torso forward, moving the chest towards the thighs.

3. Gently drop the arms down and place the palms by the sides of the feet.

4. Stay here and breathe for 30 seconds to 1 minute.

5. Lift the head up, take a breath here, inhale, and come back to Tadasana.

Joint Actions:

- Forward flexion of the spine.
- Neutral hip with anterior pelvic tilt.
- Extension of knees with a neutral ankle.
- Flexion of shoulders with elbow extension.
- Extension of wrists.

Main Muscle Actions:

- It stretches the gastrocnemius, hamstrings, gluteal group of muscles, and lower lumbar muscles.
- Contraction of the lumbar spinal flexor muscle group.

Things To Focus On:

- Focus on creating a firm base by spreading the toes wide and pressing them on the mat; place the soles of the feet firmly on the ground; and engage the large muscles in the thighs and lower leg.
- Focus on internally rotating the hips, engaging the core by drawing the navel in, and maintaining length in the spine as you fold forward.

Things To Be Cared For:

- People with recent abdominal surgeries and women during their pregnancy and menstrual cycle should avoid practicing this pose.
- People with back injuries, high blood pressure, and lumbar issues should practice this under the supervision of a therapeutic yoga teacher.

Padahastasana Variation 1

Padahastasana Variation 2

2. Parivrtta Trikonasana (Revolved Triangle Pose):

Steps To Perform:

1. Stand in Tadasana and spread the legs 3 to 4 feet apart, palms on the hips.
2. Turn the right foot 90 degrees, the left foot inwards 60 degrees to the right, squaring the hips.
3. Inhale, lift the left hand up towards the ceiling, exhale, start bending forward, twisting the torso to the right, bring the left palm on top of the right foot, stretch the right hand up towards the ceiling, and gaze at the right thumb.
4. Stay and breathe here for 30 seconds to 1 minute.
5. Inhale, come up, and repeat on the other side.

Joint Actions:

- Slight flexion and adduction of the hips on the front leg.
- Slight extension and internal rotation of the hips on the back leg.
- Extension of the knees.
- Neutral spine.
- Forward flexion and lateral rotation of the lumbar spine.
- Lateral rotation of the cervical spine.
- Abduction of shoulders with elbow extension.

Main Muscle Actions:

- It stretches the quadratus lumborum and external abdominal oblique muscles.
- It stretches the pectoral muscles.
- Contraction of the rectus and transversus abdominis muscles.
- It stretches the gastrocnemius and hamstring muscles.

Things To Focus On:

- Engage the feet by spreading and pressing the toes, soles, and heels of the feet firmly on the mat.
- Engage the hip flexors, draw the navel in, and tuck the tailbone to engage the core as you twist the torso.
- Focus on engaging the shoulders by moving the shoulder blades away from each other and stretching the arms, keeping the shoulders in line.

Things To Be Cared For:

- People suffering from migraines, hip, neck, knee, shoulder, back, or spine injuries and with recent abdominal, brain, or heart surgeries should practice this pose under the supervision of a therapeutic yoga teacher.
- Women should avoid this pose during pregnancy and menstrual cycles.

Parivritta Trikonasana Variation 1

Parivritta Trikonasana Variation 2

3. Ardha Pasasana (Half Moose Pose):

Steps To Perform:

1. Sit in a deep squat position with the feet and knees together.
2. Inhale, lengthen the spine, bring the right upper arm close to the left knee, and rest the right hand by the side of the left leg. Place the left hand behind the left buttock, exhale, and twist the torso towards the left.
3. Stay here and breathe for 30 seconds to 1 minute.
4. Inhale and come back to a deep squat.
5. Repeat the same on the right side.

Joint Actions:

- Flexion and adduction of the hips
- Posterior pelvic tilt of the hip.
- Lateral rotation of the spine.
- Slight flexion and adduction of the bent arm.
- Slight extension and adduction of the extended arm.
- Flexion of the elbow on the bent arm.
- Extension of the elbow on the extended arm.
- Flexion of the knees.
- Neutral ankles.

Main Muscle Action:

- Contraction of intertransverse, lateralis, quadratus lumborum, and interspinales muscles.
- Contraction of the iliac, psoas, and rectus femoris muscles.
- It stretches the gluteal and lower lumbar muscle groups.

Things To Focus On:

- Engage the toes, heels, and soles of the feet by firmly pressing them on the mat.
- Engage the core by drawing the navel in as you begin to twist the torso.
- Focus on firmly pressing the armpit against the outer edge of the knee and using this pressure to try to lengthen the spine.

Things To Be Cared For:

- People suffering from hip, knee, shoulder, back, or spine injuries or recent abdominal, brain, or heart surgeries should practice these asanas under the supervision of a therapeutic yoga teacher.
- People suffering from abdominal hernia or herniated disks or pregnant women should avoid practicing this pose.

Ardha Pashasana Variation 1

4. Pashu Vishram Asana (Animal Relaxing Pose):

Steps To Perform:

1. Sit in Dandasana, bend the left knee, and place the left heel against the right thigh close to the perineum.
2. Bend the right knee and place the right heel by the side of the right buttock.
3. Inhale, lengthen the spine, extend the arms over the head, exhale, fold forward, and bring the forehead down on the mat with the arms extended in front of the head.
4. Stay and breathe here for 30 seconds to 2 minutes.
5. Inhale and come up; repeat the same on the other side by interchanging the legs.

Joint Actions:

- Flexion, adduction, and internal rotation of the right hip with the right knee moved towards the left.
- Flexion, adduction, and internal rotation of the left hip with the left knee moved towards the right.
- Flexion of the lumbar spine.
- Complete flexion of the shoulders with elbow extension and forearm pronation.
- Plantarflexion of the ankles.

Main Muscle Actions:

- Contraction of hip flexors (Iliacus, iliopsoas, and rectus femoris) muscles.
- Contraction of the rectus and transversus abdominis muscles.
- Contraction of the hamstrings and gastrocnemius muscles.
- Contraction of cervical flexors.
- It stretches the erector spinae muscle.

Things To Focus On:

- Engage the core by drawing the navel in; engage the obliques as you start bending laterally to one side.
- Keep your neck relaxed.

Things To Be Cared For:

- People who have serious lower back injuries, hypertension, or hip injuries should practice under the supervision of a therapeutic yoga teacher.
- Women should avoid practicing this pose during pregnancy.

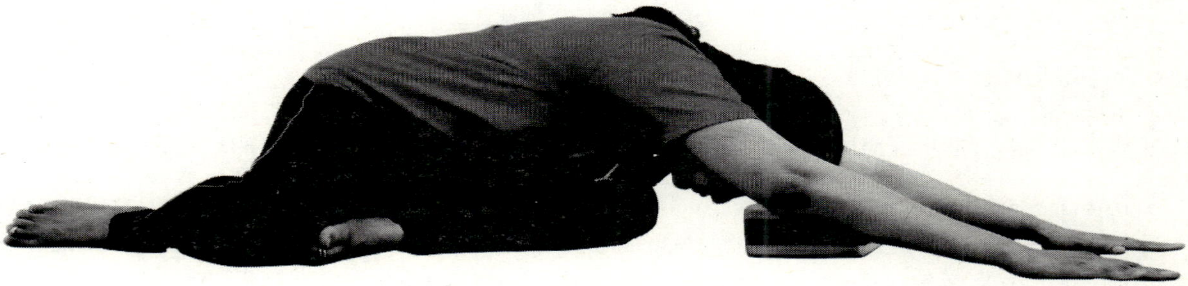

Pashu Vishramasana Variation 1

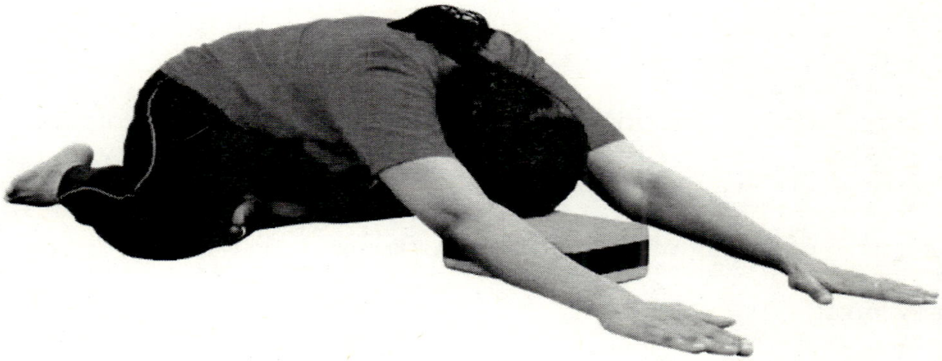

Pashu Vishramasana Variation Side View

5. Malasana (Garland Pose):

Steps To Perform:

1. Stand in Tadasana, spread the feet mat width apart, and sit in a deep squat position.
2. Bring the upper arms between the legs, bend the elbows, place the upper arms on the inner edges of the calf muscle, palms in Anjali Mudra (prayer position), and keep pushing the knees outwards, maintaining the back straight, gazing forward.
3. Stay and breathe here for 30 seconds to 1 minute.
4. Inhale and come back to Tadasana.

Joint Actions:

- Neutral spine.
- Flexion of hips, with posterior pelvic tilt, abduction, and external rotation.
- Flexion of the knees in a neutral position.
- Slight abduction of the shoulders with elbow flexion and wrist extension.

Main Muscle Actions:

- It stretches the hip adductor groups.
- Contraction of the hip flexors and knee flexors muscle groups.
- Contraction of the rectus abdominis and transversus abdominis muscle groups.

Things To Focus On:

- Engage the feet by spreading and pressing the toes, soles, and heels of the feet completely on the mat.

- Engage the hip flexor, thighs, and glutes, and engage the core by drawing the navel in and tucking the tailbone to bring the buttocks close to the mat, keeping the length in the spine.
- Engage the shoulders by drawing the shoulder blades closer, and engage the elbows by pressing them against the inner edges of the knees to abduct the hips.

Things To Be Cared For:

- People suffering from hip, knee, shoulder, back, or spine injuries and with recent abdominal, brain, or heart surgeries, or women during pregnancy, should practice this pose under the supervision of a therapeutic yoga teacher

Malasana Variation 1

Malasana Variation 2

6. Chakki Chalanasana (Churning the Mill Pose):

Steps To Perform:

1. Sit in Dandasana and stretch the legs out in front of the body as wide as possible.
2. Interlock the fingers and hold the arms straight in front of the chest.
3. Start to rotate the waist in a circular motion, exhaling while bending forward and inhaling while leaning back, moving the hands over the right and left feet to complete a circle.
4. Practice 5 to 10 rounds clockwise and anti-clockwise.

Joint Actions:

- Flexion and complete abduction of the hips.
- Knee extension and ankle dorsiflexion.
- Lateral flexion and forward flexion of the spine.
- Flexion of shoulders and extension of elbows.

Main Muscle Actions:

- It stretches the hip adductor muscle group.
- It contracts and stretches the quadratus lumborum and intertransverse lateralis muscles.
- Contracts the quadriceps femoris muscles.

Things To Focus On:

- Engage the core by drawing the navel in, and keep the spine erect.
- Engage the shoulders by stretching the arms forward and interlocking the palms, keeping them in line with the shoulders.
- Engage the hip flexors as you begin to rotate the hips, keeping the upper body steady and the core engaged.
- Focus on keeping the knees and elbows straight throughout the practice.

Things To Be Cared For:

- People suffering from hip, knee, shoulder, back, or spine injuries and those who have undergone recent abdominal, brain, or heart surgeries should practice this pose under the supervision of a therapeutic yoga teacher.

Chakki Chalanasana Variation 1 Left

Chakki Chalanasana Variation 1 Right

7. Urdhva Pada: Hasta Namanasana (Lifted Leg and Hand Salute):

Steps To Perform:

1. Sit in Dandasana with the legs stretched out.
2. Bend the knees, keeping the feet together away from the buttocks.
3. Inhale, lengthen the spine, and hug the thighs with both hands as you exhale.
4. Inhale and lift the legs, bringing them parallel to the floor with bent knees. Draw the knees close to the chest, bringing the hands between the thighs and palms in Anjali Mudra (prayer pose) in front of the chest.
5. Stay and breathe here for 30 seconds to 1 minute.
6. Exhale and release.

Joint Actions:

- Mild lumbar spinal flexion with the thoracic and cervical spines in a neutral position.
- Flexion of the hip with adduction.
- Flexion of the knee with ankle plantar flexion.
- Mild abduction and internal rotation of the shoulders.
- Elbow flexion with wrist extension.

Main Muscle Actions:

- Contraction of the rectus, transverse abdominis, and hip flexors.
- Contraction of the extensor group of muscles in the back.
- Contraction of the deltoids and bicep muscles.

➢ It stretches the lower lumbar and gluteal muscles.

Things To Focus On:

➢ Engage the core by drawing your navel in. Focus on engaging the shoulders by lifting them and locking the hands behind the thighs, hugging the legs. Try to keep the spine erect, resisting flexion.

Things To Be Cared For:

➢ People suffering from hip, knee, shoulder, back, or spine injuries and those with recent abdominal, brain, or heart surgeries should practice this asana under the supervision of a therapeutic yoga teacher.

➢ Women should avoid practicing this pose during pregnancy and menstrual cycles.

Urdhva Pada Hasta Namanasana Variation 1

Urdhva Pada Hasta Namanasana Variation 2

8. Bhu Namanasana (Greeting the Earth Pose):

Steps To Perform:

1. Sit in Dandasana.
2. Bring the arms parallel to the floor, inhale, exhale, and twist the torso to the left, placing the palms behind the body.
3. Try to place the forehead between the palms.
4. Stay here and breathe for 30 seconds to 1 minute.
5. Inhale, come back to Dandasana, and repeat on the other side.

Joint Actions:

- Lateral rotation of the spine.
- Flexion of the cervical spine with lateral rotation.
- Adduction of the hips.
- Extension of the knees.
- Dorsiflexion of the ankles.
- Slight flexion of the shoulder and adduction.
- Flexion of the elbow with pronation of the forearm.
- Extension of the wrist of the upper arm.

Main Muscle Actions:

- It stretches and contracts the intertransverse lateralis, quadratus lumborum, and interspinales.
- Contraction of the levator scapulae and sternocleidomastoid muscles of the neck.

Things To Focus On:

- Engage the core by drawing the navel in as you begin to twist the torso.

- Focus on engaging the arms by pressing the palms and fingers firmly on the mat.
- Keep the spine as straight as possible.

Things To Be Cared For:

- People suffering from hip, knee, shoulder, back, or spine injuries, or those who have undergone recent abdominal, brain, or heart surgeries, should practice this pose under the supervision of a therapeutic yoga teacher.
- Women should avoid practicing this pose during pregnancy or the menstrual cycle.

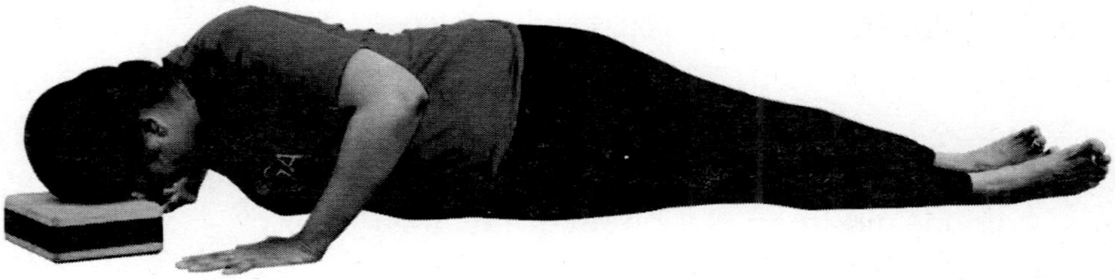

Bhoonamanasana Variation 1

9. Pada Hasta Sanchalanasana (Supine Cycling—Arms and Legs):

Steps To Perform:

1. Lie on your back.
2. Bend the knees and raise the feet off the floor, keeping the calves parallel to the floor.
3. Reach the arms forward and place them along the thighs.
4. Start paddling the legs and arms forward (alternate arm and leg).
5. Repeat this movement at least 15 times.

Joint Actions:

- Flexion, adduction, and internal rotation of the hips.
- Neutral spine.
- Flexion and extension of elbows.
- Flexion and extension of the knees.
- Plantar flexion of the ankles.

Main Muscle Actions:

- Contraction of the rectus and transversus abdominis muscle groups.
- Contraction of the hip and knee flexor muscle groups (hamstrings) along with the extensors of the knee muscle group (quadriceps femoris).

Things To Focus On:

- Focus on keeping the shoulders and core muscles active, and squeeze the thighs to activate the quads.
- Focus on keeping the pelvis neutral on the mat.

Things To Be Cared For:

- People suffering from shoulder, back, or neck pain should practice this pose under the supervision of a therapeutic yoga teacher.
- Women should avoid practicing this pose during pregnancy or the menstrual cycle.

Treatment for Acidity & Gastritis:

Ayurveda:

- **Nidan Parivarjan:** withdrawal of the etiological factors of the disease.
- **Samshodana Chikitsa**: Vamana and Virechana are considered the best treatments for Amla Pitta by Acharya Kashyapa.

Allopathy:

For acidity, allopathic medications may include:

- Antacids.
- H2 Receptor.
- Aluminum and magnesium antacids are proton-pump inhibitors.

In more severe conditions, doctors may suggest surgery.

For gastritis or gastric issues, depending on the cause, treatment may include:

- Antacids.
- Antibiotics.
- Proton pump inhibitors.
- H2 blockers.
- Antinausea medication.

Pranayama:

- Abdominal breathing.
- Viloma pranayama (3 levels).
- Kapalabhati.
- Kaki pranayama.
- Swana pranayama.
- Bhramari pranayama.

Nutrition for Acidity & Gastritis:

Acidity is inconvenient for the sufferer and those around them. Constant burping, or flatulence, creates an unhealthy environment. A good diet significantly reduces acidity. Healthy eating should be a lifestyle, not just a temporary cure, as acidity or gastritis don't vanish overnight. There's a high chance of a recurrence if unhealthy habits return.

Foods to Consume:

Fibrous Food	Food that is high in fiber makes you feel fuller, so you are less likely to overeat
Whole Grain	Oats / steel cut oats, brown rice, quinoa, whole wheat flour, barley, buckwheat, ragi/ finger millet
Vegetables	Cooked beetroot, carrots, sweet potatoes, spinach, fenugreek, broccoli, cucumber
Non-Citrus Fruits	Bananas, melons, papayas, apples
Lean Protein	Tofu, paneer, chicken breast, egg whites
Nuts & Seeds	Almonds, chia seeds, flax seeds, peanuts when taken in moderation can help in absorbing stomach acids and provide healthy fats and nutrients
Unsaturated Fats	Avocados, walnuts, olive oil
Others	Prebiotics and probiotics can help in building good gut bacteria which aid in better digestion; Ghee - helps to improve digestion and acts as a lubricant for the gut; Drinking 2 to 3 liters of water in a day; Ginger

- Moderation is key; avoid problematic foods, especially before bedtime.
- Opt for small, frequent meals instead of large ones.
- Avoid late-night dinners.
- Steer clear of snacking between meals.
- Stay adequately hydrated.
- Add a pinch of asafoetida to buttermilk to reduce bloating.

Foods to Avoid:

Acidic Food	Tomatoes, pineapple, vinegar, onions, oranges, lime, berries, pomegranates
Raw Vegetables	Carrots, beetroots, brussels sprouts, cabbage, radish, asparagus, garlic
Caffeinated Beverages	Coffee, tea, energy drinks
Carbonated Beverages	Sodas

Foods With Excess Sodium & Sugar	Candies, chips, canned food etc.
Processed Food	White bread, cakes, other store bought or bakery products
Spicy Food	Chilis, jalapenos, excess use of pepper
Unsaturated Fats	Avocados, walnuts, olive oil
Others	Oily food/ deep fried food, fatty meat, mint, alcohol, and smoking; intolerant foods like Dairy, Gluten etc. - This depends on how one feels after consumption. If any food causes bloating, it's best to be avoided.

- Identify and eliminate foods causing uneasiness or triggering acidity.
- Eat on time; avoid starving to prevent excess stomach acid, acid reflux, and nausea.

Minor lifestyle changes, like incorporating physical exercises (walking, jogging, yoga), go a long way. Yoga practice helps relieve bloating, enhances digestion, and promotes internal cleansing through kriyas. Daily pranayama, guided properly, improves immunity, lung capacity, and provides relief from allergies.

DIABETES

PANCREAS ANATOMY

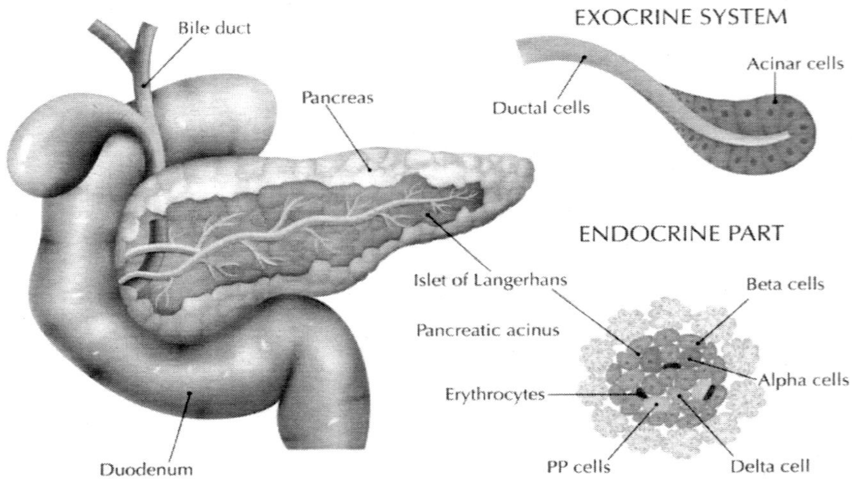

Diabetes is a chronic condition wherein the pancreas, responsible for producing the endocrine hormone insulin, starts malfunctioning. Due to this malfunction, insulin may either be completely absent, insufficient, or not utilized properly by the body, leading to increased glucose levels in the blood (hyperglycemia).

When a person is diagnosed with diabetes and is not treated or cared for properly, it can lead to various other health issues such as diabetic retinopathy, diabetic neuropathy, frozen shoulder, cardiovascular disease, PCOS/PCOD, etc.

The most common types of diabetes found in individuals are:

1. **Type 1 Diabetes:** Also known as insulin-dependent diabetes mellitus (IDDM), this condition is characterized by either reduced or completely absent insulin production. It is commonly observed in children between the ages of 10 and 19.

2. **Type 2 Diabetes:** Referred to as Non-Insulin Dependent Diabetes Mellitus (NIDDM), this condition arises when the body becomes resistant to insulin, rendering the pancreas unable to produce sufficient insulin. It is commonly seen in adults.

3. **Gestational Diabetes:** This condition can be observed in some pregnant women with high blood sugar levels. There is a possibility that these women will develop type 2 diabetes even after giving birth.

4. **Prediabetes:** This condition indicates elevated blood sugar levels, not high enough for a type 2 diabetes diagnosis. It serves as an alert for individuals to adopt a proper diet and exercise to maintain a healthy weight and avoid developing diabetes in the future.

According to Ayurveda, prameha (pre-diabetes) is characterized by excessive urination and other abnormal qualities resulting from an imbalance of the doshas. Foods that increase Kapha, Medha, and Moothra act as etiological factors for Prameha. Kapha imbalance spreads throughout the body, mixing with Medas (adipose tissue), Mamsa (flesh), and Kleda (body fluids), leading to Prameha.

Ayurveda identifies two ways in which Prameha can develop: either due to the loss of tissues in the body (dhatus) or due to blockages caused by one dosha or dhatu affecting the others (srotas). According to Ayurveda, there are 20 types of Prameha, and if left untreated, it can progress to Madhumeha (diabetes mellitus).

According to Ayurvedic texts, some causes of Prameha (pre-diabetes) include excessive consumption of heavy-to-digest (guru), sour (amla), salty (lavana rasa), or greasy (snigdha) foods, lack of exercise (avyayama), lack of mental exercise (achinta), and excessive sleep (atinidra).

Causes:

When the body's immune system, responsible for fighting infections, starts destroying the beta cells in the pancreas (crucial for insulin production), it results in the complete failure of insulin secretion. This process leads to type 2 diabetes.

Additionally, when the body is unable to utilize insulin effectively, the demand for insulin to facilitate glucose entry into cells becomes overwhelming. Initially, the pancreas increases insulin secretion to meet this additional demand. However, over time, it fails to produce enough insulin, resulting in elevated glucose levels and the onset of type 2 diabetes. Lack of exercise, being overweight, and obesity can contribute to this condition.

Gestational diabetes, observed in some pregnant women, is primarily due to hormonal changes combined with genetic factors and an abnormal weight gain during pregnancy.

Symptoms:

- Dehydration is caused by increased glucose in the urine, leading to frequent urination.
- Thirst, appetite, dry mouth.
- Weight loss or gain, fatigue, nausea, blurred vision, and vomiting.
- Frequent infections: respiratory, gastrointestinal, and genitourinary.
- Abnormal sensations like pins and needles in the feet or toes.
- Wounds that do not heal quickly.
- Lethargy and unconsciousness when glucose levels are extremely elevated.

Diagnosis:

Various tests can determine diabetes:

- **FBS:** Done before consuming food (fasting).
- **PPBS:** Done after having food.
- **RPG:** Random Plasma Glucose.
- **HbA1c:** Hemoglobin A1c test.

Results are interpreted based on the following values:

- **Normal:** 70 mg/dL–100 mg/dL
- **Prediabetes:** 100 mg/dL–125 mg/dL
- **Diabetes:** 126 mg/dL or higher.

Yogic Intervention:

Yoga is an ancient art that originated in our country more than 5000 years ago and has proven to be a perfect tool in balancing and integrating the body, mind and emotions. The practice of Yoga is beneficial in the management of several diseases. Type 2 diabetes is also one among them. Researchers have found out that a group of people those who are diabetics are being introduced a Yogic regimen comprised with strict diet plan, asana, Pranayama, Bandhas, meditation, has a tremendous effect in bringing the glycaemic levels under control which in turn reducing the risk of further complications arising out of diabetes.

Yoga, as therapy which is still a very new concept but gaining momentum is developing a new horizon in the healthcare system.

Yoga practice is so practical that it promotes the use of vegetable and fruit in abundance in the dietary plans promoting a perfect balanced eating habits replacing the harmful junk foods. And in the process enabling them to lose weight adequately and having control of glycaemic levels.

The Yoga regimen should be designed according to the needs of an individual after coming to know their health condition, requirement, complications, risk factors etc. After evaluating all these the Yoga Therapist decides whether the individual should be introduced to a low intensity or a high intensity practice.

Yoga is a cost - effective way to treat diabetes. Several studies on yoga in the management of diabetes suggest that with the combination of mind – body therapies, it has the ability to reduce stress related hyperglycemia and shown a positive effect in controlling blood glucose level.

Case Study:

Subjective: Mr Ramesh (name changed), a 58 year old walked into our yoga center in the year 2007. He enquired about any remedies for excessive perspiration and fatigue. We asked him to get his blood test done.

Objective: Ramesh had high blood sugar and had visited a doctor who prescribed him diabetic medications and suggested he should have regular exercises.

Assessment: Ramesh came back to our center with his blood report and we suggested he join our regular class.

Plan: Ramesh practiced in our regular class for about six weeks and found improvement in his condition. He even joined the therapy yoga for 10 sessions and found it extremely helpful in managing his diabetes.

He still practices under our supervision and has been managing his diabetes well within normal range with no further diabetic comorbidities.

- **Surya Namaskar (Sun Salutations):**

Regular practice of Surya Namaskars can be beneficial.

- **Asanas (Yoga Postures):**

The following are some postures that are helpful in managing diabetes:

1. Parivrtta Utkatasana (Revolved Chair Pose):

Steps To Perform:

1. Stand in Tadasana with the feet, toes, and heels together.

2. Inhale, lift the spine, and stretch both arms up.

3. Exhale, bend the knees, and push the buttocks back and down as though sitting on an imaginary chair.

4. Inhale, while exhaling, twist the torso towards the right, bring the left elbow to the outer side of the right thigh, gently place the right palm on top of the left, as in Anjali Mudra, with the right elbow pointing towards the ceiling, and gaze up towards the ceiling.

5. Stay and breathe here for 30 seconds to 1 minute.

6. Inhale, come out of the pose, and repeat on the other side.

Joint Actions:

- Rotation of the spine.
- Flexion of the hips.
- Adduction and medial rotation of the knees.
- Flexion of the shoulders.
- Flexion of the elbows.
- Supination of the forearms.
- Flexion of the knees.
- Dorsiflexion of the ankles.

Main Muscle Actions:

- Contraction of the quadratus lumborum, rectus, and transversus abdominis muscles.
- Contraction of iliacus and psoas major and hamstring muscles.
- Stretching of the gluteus, internal, and external muscles.

Things To Focus On:

- Engage the muscles in the thighs and spread the toes equally to create a stable base.
- Focus on keeping the knees and feet together by pressing the thighs against each other.
- Focus on keeping the knees in line with the toes; push the buttocks back and down; the knees should not go beyond the toes; and bring the thighs almost parallel to the floor.
- Engage the core by drawing the navel in while lowering the buttocks and keeping the spine lifted and shoulders relaxed.
- Engage the shoulder blades by bringing them closer while twisting to keep the chest open and create space to breathe.

Things To Be Cared For:

- People suffering from chronic inflammatory digestive issues, hernias, low blood pressure, or injuries to the feet or ankles should avoid practicing this pose.
- Those who have headaches, insomnia, breathing problems, chronic knee pain, or knee injuries should practice this pose under the supervision of a therapeutic yoga teacher.
- Women should avoid practicing this pose during pregnancy or the menstrual cycle.

Parivritta Utkatasana Variation 1

Parivritta Utkatasana Variation 2

2. Parivrtta Parsvakonasana (Revolved Side Angle Pose):

Steps To Perform:

1. Stand in Tadasana and spread the feet 4 to 4.5 feet apart, pointing the toes forward.
2. Turn the right foot 90 degrees to the right, the left foot 30 to 60 degrees inward, and square the hips.
3. Exhale, bend the right knee, bring the right knee in line with the right ankle, sink the hips, and bring the right thigh parallel to the floor.
4. Inhale, lean forward towards the right foot, place the left elbow on the outer side of the right thigh, exhale, and twist the spine towards the right side.
5. Gently place the right palm on top of the left in Anjali Mudra, with the right elbow pointing towards the ceiling, and gaze up at the right shoulder.
6. Stay and breathe here for 30 seconds to 1 minute.
7. Come out of the pose and repeat it on the other side.

Joint Actions:

- Axial rotation of the spine.
- Extension and adduction of the hip on the back leg.
- Flexion of the hip on the front leg.
- Downward rotation and abduction of the scapular.
- Flexion and adduction of the shoulder.
- Flexion of the elbow.
- Pronation of the forearm.
- Flexion of the knee on the front leg.
- Dorsiflexion of the ankle on the front leg.
- Extension of the knee on the back leg.
- Dorsiflexion of the ankle on the back leg.

Main Muscle Actions:

- Contraction of the iliacus and psoas major of the forward leg.
- Contraction of the hamstring of the forward leg.
- Stretching of the hamstring and gastrocnemius of the backward leg.
- Contraction and stretching of the quadratus lumborum and internal and external oblique muscles.

Things To Focus On:

- Focus on pressing the soles of the feet firmly on the mat to create a stable base.
- Focus on engaging the hip flexor while bending the knee and sinking the hips, keeping the pelvis level.
- Focus on aligning the front knee over the ankle and the thigh parallel to the floor by engaging the hips and quads.
- Bring the elbow outside the bent knee, focus on engaging the core by drawing the navel in, and keep the spine lifted.
- Engage the quads, hamstrings, and hip flexors while getting into the twist, and keep the neck neutral.

Things To Be Cared For:

- People suffering from high blood pressure, migraines, hip, knee, or neck injuries should avoid practicing this pose.
- Women should avoid practicing this pose during pregnancy and menstrual cycles.

Parivritta Parsvakonasana Variation 1 Left

Parivritta Parsvakonasana Variation 1 Right

3. Sarpasana (Snake Pose):

Steps To Perform:

1. Lie on the belly, place the palms by the side of the thighs, join the feet together, and press the toes firmly on the mat.
2. Roll the shoulders back, clasp the palms behind the back, and firmly press them against each other.
3. Inhale and lift the head and chest up until the last rib.
4. Exhale; pull the palms away from the buttocks.
5. Stay and breathe here for 30 seconds to 1 minute.
6. Exhale and release.

Joint Actions:

- Extension of the spine.
- Extension and adduction of the hips.
- Extension of the elbows.
- Extension of the knees.
- Plantarflexion of the ankles.
- Downward rotation, adduction of the scapula.

Main Muscle Actions:

- Contraction of the erector spinae, retractors of the scapula, and gluteus maximus muscles.
- Stretching of pectoral, rectus, and transversus abdominis muscles.

Things To Focus On:

- Engage the core by drawing the navel in, squeeze the glutes and push them down, and engage the thighs by pressing them against each other.

- Focus on pressing the toes on the mat and keep stretching them, keeping the feet together.
- Engage the shoulder blades by rolling them back and down, bringing them closer to each other, and stretching the ribs outward while lifting the head and chest.
- Keep the neck neutral and follow thoracic breathing to stay in the pose by making use of the chest to breathe.

Things To Be Cared For:

- People who have undergone recent abdominal surgery or have injuries to the hip, knee, neck, shoulder, or spine, or people suffering from hernia, peptic ulcer, and intestinal tuberculosis, should avoid practicing this pose.
- People suffering from heart problems should practice this pose under the supervision of a therapeutic yoga teacher.
- Women should avoid practicing this pose during pregnancy and menstrual cycles.

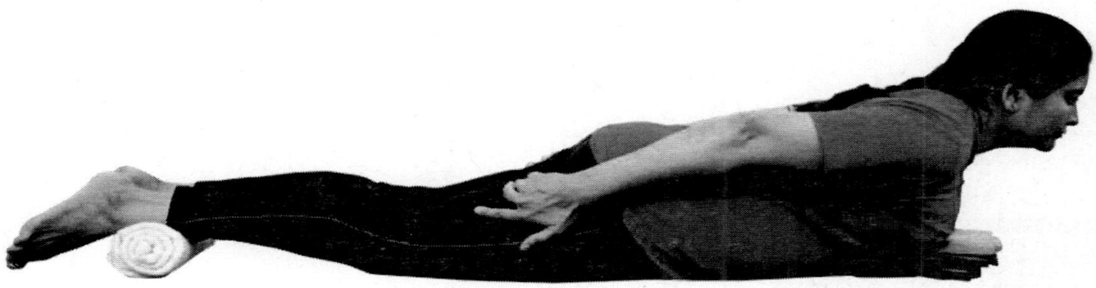

Sarpasana Variation 1

Sarpasana Variation 2

4. Shalabasana (Locust Pose):

Steps To Perform:

1. Lie on the belly with the feet together, toes and heels touching each other.
2. Rest the chin or forehead on the mat, and place the palms under the thighs.
3. Inhale and lift the legs and thighs, keeping the knees straight.
4. Stay and breathe here for 30 seconds to 1 minute.
5. Exhale and release.

Joint Actions:

- Flexion of the spine.
- Extension and adduction of the hips.
- Backward rotation and adduction of the scapula.
- Flexion of the shoulders.
- Extension of the elbows.
- Extension of the knees.
- Plantar flexion of the ankles.

Main Muscle Actions:

- Contraction of the gluteus and erector spinae muscles.
- Contraction of gastrocnemius muscles.
- Stretching of the hip flexor muscle group.

Things To Focus On:

- Engage the core by drawing the navel in, squeezing the glutes, pushing them down, and engaging the thighs and legs while lifting the legs.

- Focus on internally rotating the thighs and hips by engaging the hip flexors.
- Focus on straightening the knees, and keep stretching the toes by pointing them back.
- Keep the neck relaxed and stable.

Things To Be Cared For:

- People suffering from recent hip, knee, neck, shoulder, spine, abdominal surgeries, or people having hernia, peptic ulcer, and intestinal tuberculosis should avoid practicing this pose.
- People suffering from heart problems, lumbar issues, or lower back pain should practice this pose under the supervision of a therapeutic yoga teacher.
- Women should avoid practicing this pose during pregnancy and menstrual cycles.

Shalabasana Variation 1

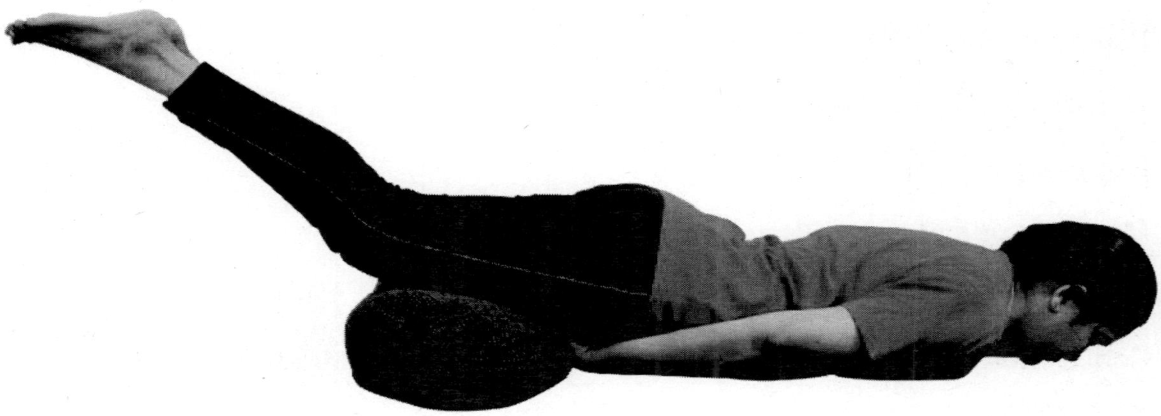

Shalabasana Variation 2

5. Parivrtta Bhujangasana (Revolved Cobra Pose):

Steps To Perform:

1. Lie on the belly with the feet trunk-width apart, toes pointing back, palms beside the chest, and tuck the elbows in.
2. Inhale, lift the head and chest up, roll the shoulders back and down, and push the chest forward.
3. Exhale, turn the head towards the right, gently twist the spine, keep the chin above the shoulder, and try to gaze at the right heel.
4. Stay and breathe here for 30 seconds to 1 minute.
5. Come out of the pose and repeat it on the other side.

Joint Actions:

- Extension and adduction of the hip.
- Extension of the spine.
- Downward rotation and adduction of the shoulders.
- Extension of the elbow.
- Dorsiflexion of the wrists.
- Extension of the knees.
- Plantarflexion of the ankles.

Main Muscle Actions:

- Contraction of erector spinae and gluteal muscles, and quadratus lumborum muscles.
- Stretching of hip flexors, rectus, and transversus abdominis muscles.

Things To Focus On:

- Engage the glutes by squeezing and pushing them down, engage the thighs by pressing them together, engage the lower back and core by drawing the navel in, and keep pressing and stretching the toes on the mat.
- Press the palms firmly and work on engaging the muscles in the upper arms to roll the shoulders back and stabilize the shoulders to help lift the trunk up.
- Expand the rib cage by pushing the chest forward without shrugging the shoulders.
- Focus on keeping the chin above the shoulder during the twist.

Things To Be Cared For:

- People suffering from hernia, peptic ulcer, and intestinal tuberculosis, or who have undergone recent abdominal surgeries and have injuries to the hip, knee, neck, shoulder, or spine, should avoid practicing this pose.
- People suffering from heart problems, shoulder, or neck pain should practice this pose under the supervision of a therapeutic yoga teacher.
- Women should avoid practicing this pose during pregnancy and menstrual cycles.

Pariviritta Bhujangasana Variation 1

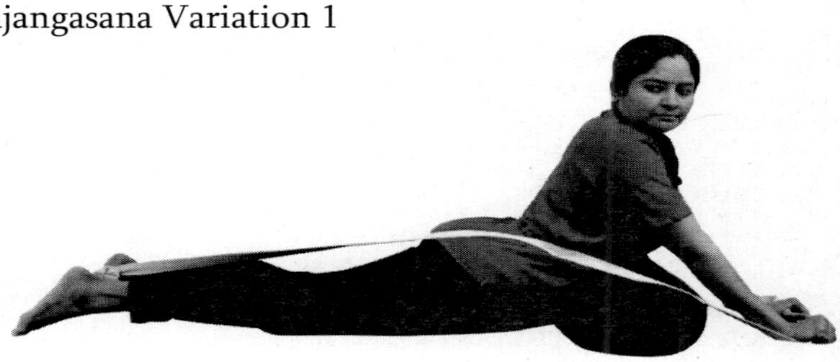

Pariviritta Bhujangasana Variation 2

6. Mandukasana (Frog Pose):

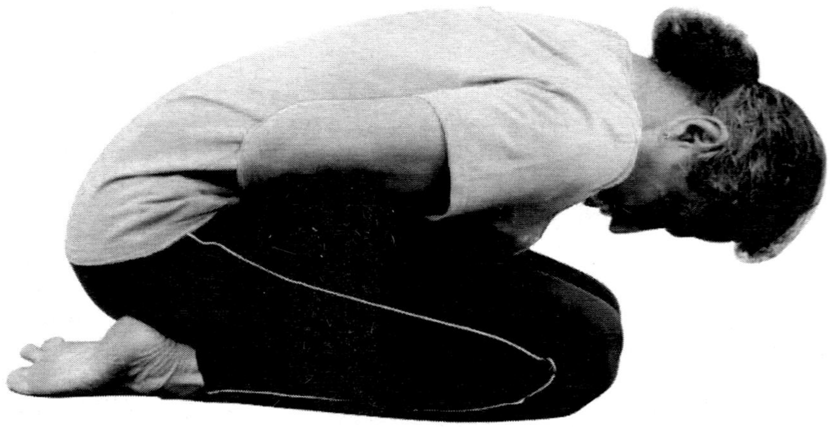

Steps To Perform:

1. Sit in Vajrasana, make fists of the palms, and place them on the belly.
2. Inhale, lift the spine, press the fists gently on the belly button, exhale, draw the navel in, and push the torso forward, feeling the pressure on the abdomen.
3. Keep gazing downward and holding your breath for 20 to 30 seconds.
4. Inhale and come back to Vajrasana.

Joint Actions:

- Flexion and adduction of the hips.
- Mild flexion of the spine.
- Downward rotation and abduction of the scapula.
- Flexion and adduction of the shoulders.
- Flexion of the elbows.
- Flexion of the knees.
- Plantarflexion of the ankles.

Main Muscle Actions:

- Contraction of the rectus and transversus abdominis muscles.
- Contraction of the hip flexors and knee flexor group of muscles.
- Stretching of the gluteus and erector spinae muscles.

Things To Focus On:

- Engage the core by drawing the navel while folding forward.
- Focus on keeping the neck neutral without dropping the chin.

Things To Be Cared For:

- People suffering from peptic or duodenal ulcers, recent abdominal surgery, stomach aches, diarrhea, spinal, hip, and neck injuries, migraines, or severe headaches should avoid practicing this pose.
- People with lower back or neck pain should do this pose under the supervision of a therapeutic yoga teacher.
- Women should avoid practicing this pose during pregnancy and menstrual cycles.

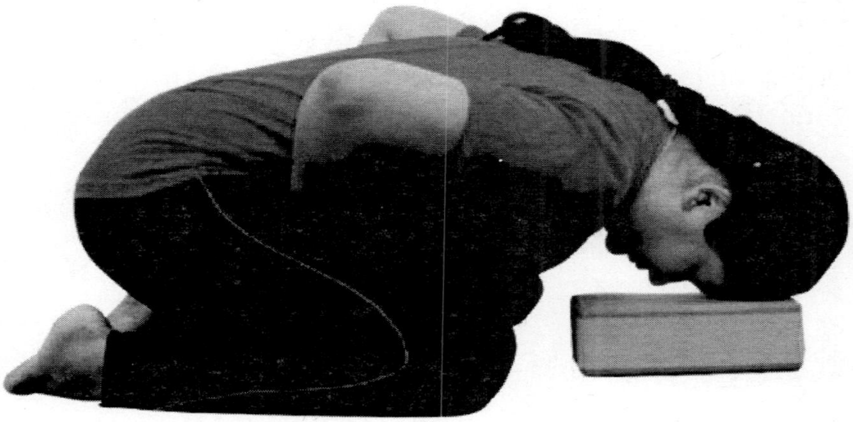

Mandukasana Variaton 1

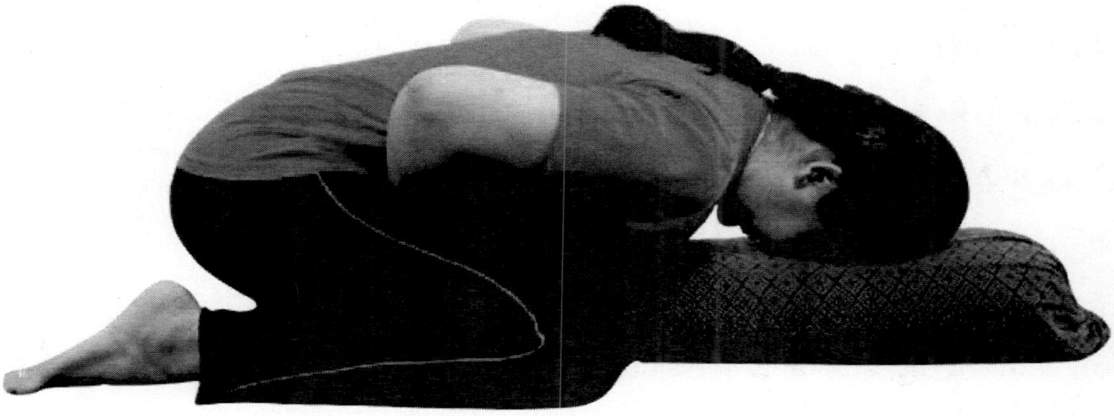

Mandukasana Variaton 2

7. Yoga Mudrasana (Yogic Seal Pose):

Steps To Perform:

1. Sit in padmasana or sukhasana.
2. Inhale, lift the spine, exhale, walk the hands forward, try to get the forehead or chin on the mat, and join the palms in Anjali mudra in front of the head.
3. Stay and breathe here for 30 seconds to 1 minute.
4. Inhale and come back to Padmasana or Sukhasana.

Joint Actions:

- Adduction and flexion of the hips.
- Mild flexion of the spine.
- Upward rotation and adduction of the shoulders.
- Abduction of the scapula.
- Extension of the elbows.
- Flexion of the knees.

Main Muscle Actions:

- Contraction of the hip and knee flexor muscle groups.
- Contraction of the rectus and transversus abdominis muscles.
- Stretching of the latissimus dorsi and gluteus maximus muscles.

Things To Focus On:

- Engage the core by drawing the navel and tailbone in and folding forward.
- Engage the hip flexors to abduct the knees, and press the thighs on the mat to keep the knees grounded.

- Focus on keeping the length in the spine throughout the pose without rounding the back.

Things To Be Cared For:

- People suffering from ankle, knee, pelvic, shoulder girdle, hip injuries, or those who have undergone recent abdominal surgeries should avoid practicing this pose.
- People with cervical and lumbar spondylosis should practice this pose under the supervision of a therapeutic yoga teacher.
- Women should avoid this pose during pregnancy and menstrual cycles.

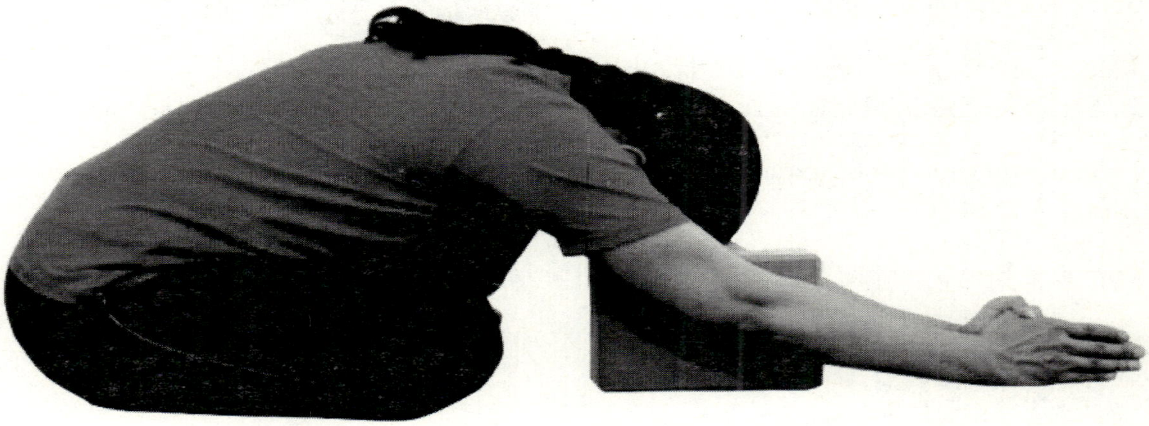

Yogamudrasana In Sukhasana Variation 1

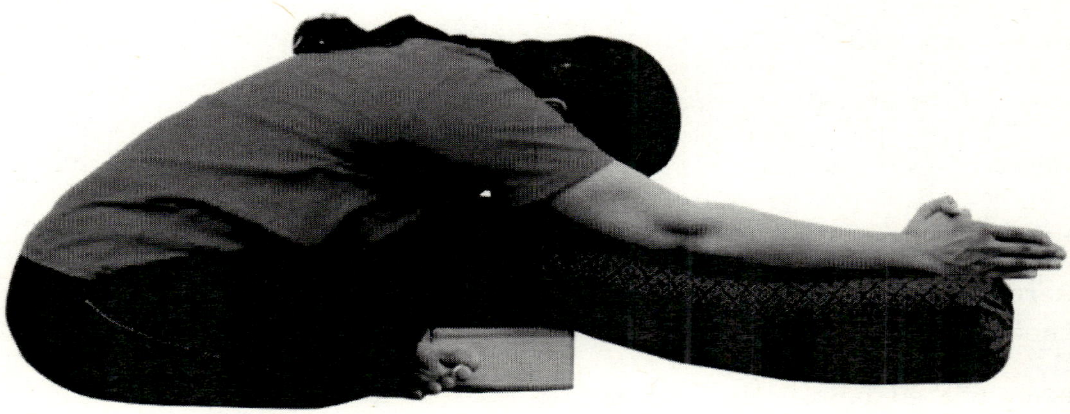

Yogamudrasana In Sukhasana Variation 2

8. Ardha Matsyendrasana (Half Lord Of The Fish Pose):

This pose is named after the great yogi Matsyendranath.

Steps To Perform:

1. Sit in Dandasana.
2. Bend the right knee and place the right heel under the left buttock.
3. Now bend the left knee and place the left ankle outside the right knee.
4. Bring the right hand over the left leg and hold the right foot.
5. Place the left palm behind the back, in between the medians of the buttocks.
6. Inhale, lift the spine, exhale, twist the torso to the left, and bring the shoulders in line.
7. Stay and breathe here for 30 seconds to 1 minute.
8. Come out of the pose and repeat it on the other side.

Joint Actions:

- Rotation of the spine towards the raised leg.
- Neutral extension of the spine.
- Deep flexion, adduction, and internal rotation of the hips on the raised leg.
- Flexion of the knee on the raised leg.
- Moderate flexion, adduction, and external rotation of the hip of the rested leg.
- Flexion of the knee on the rested leg.
- External rotation, slight abduction, and flexion move toward the extension of the glenohumeral joint on the front arm.
- Flexion of the elbow on the front arm.
- Neutral extension of the wrist on the front arm.
- External rotation is the extension of the glenohumeral joint on the back arm.
- Extension of the elbow on the back arm.

➢ Dorsiflexion of the wrist on the back arm.

Main Muscle Actions:

➢ Contraction of the iliacus and psoas major of the upward leg.

➢ Contraction of the hamstring on both legs.

➢ Stretching of the IT band, quadratus lumborum, and internal and external oblique muscles

Things To Focus On:

➢ Focus on engaging the thigh on the rested leg to rest the knee on the mat.

➢ Focus on pressing the toes on the raised leg completely on the mat, making sure the inner edge of the foot does not lift.

➢ Engage the core by drawing the navel in, engaging the hip flexor and glutes, and working on pushing the navel away from the thigh, creating enough space to breathe comfortably.

➢ While getting into the twist, work on bringing the shoulders in line and keeping the neck neutral.

Things To Be Cared For:

➢ People suffering from hip, neck, knee, shoulder, back, spine injuries, peptic ulcers, hernia, and those who have undergone recent abdominal, brain, or heart surgeries should avoid doing this pose.

➢ People with slipped discs and cervical issues should practice this pose under the supervision of a therapeutic yoga teacher.

➢ Women should avoid practicing this pose during pregnancy and menstrual cycles.

Ardha Matsyendrasna Variation 1

Ardha Matsyendrasna Variation 2

9. Marichyasana II (Sage Marichi's Twist II):

This pose is dedicated to Sage Marichi, who was the son of Brahma and the grandfather of Surya.

Steps To Perform:

1. Sit in Dandasana.
2. Bend the left knee with the foot close to the buttock.
3. Inhale, lift the spine, stretch the right hand up, bring the right elbow outside the left knee, and hold the right knee with the right hand.
4. Place the left hand in line with the left buttock.
5. Push the left knee away from the abdomen, exhale, and twist the torso towards the left.
6. Widen the chest, twist, and bring the shoulders in line with each other.
7. Stay and breathe here for 30 seconds to 1 minute.
8. Come out of the pose and repeat it on the other side.

Joint Actions:

- Flexion, external rotation, and adduction of the hip on the raised leg.
- Flexion and adduction of the hip on the extended leg.
- Rotation of the spine towards the raised leg.
- Abduction of the shoulder in the front arm.
- Flexion of the elbow in the front arm.
- Extension of the shoulder in the back arm.
- Extension of the elbow in the back arm.

- Dorsiflexion of the wrist in the back arm.
- Neutral scapula.
- Extension of the knee on the extended leg.

Main Muscle Actions:

- Contraction of the hip and knee flexor muscle groups of the bent leg.
- Stretching of the quadratus lumborum and internal and external oblique muscles.

Things To Focus On:

- Focus on internally rotating the hip to keep the pelvis level.
- Engage the shoulder blades by rolling them back and down, pushing the chest forward, and keeping the shoulders in line in the final position.
- Draw the navel in and engage the core; pull the navel region away from the thigh of the raised leg; and engage the oblique while twisting.
- Keep the neck neutral.

Things To Be Cared For:

- People suffering from hip, neck, knee, shoulder, back, or spine injuries, recent abdominal, brain, and heart surgeries, peptic ulcers, or hernias should avoid practicing this pose.
- People with a slipped disc and cervical issues should do this asana in the presence of a therapeutic yoga teacher.
- Women should avoid practicing this pose during pregnancy and menstrual cycles.

Marichyasana II Variation 1

Marichyasana II Variation 2

Treatment for Diabetes:

Ayurveda:

The treatment principles for diabetic patients can be categorized based on their body type, whether they are Sthulya (obese) or Krush (lean). For Sthulya patients, treatment should focus on the proper utilization of excess fat, including a purification process (Shodhana), reduction of body weight through diet, drugs, and exercises (Apatarpan), emesis therapy (Vamana), therapeutic purgation (Virechana), and application of medicine through the anal route (Basti).

For Krush patients, an aesthetic type of treatment should be given to increase stamina and vitality through the use of tonics (brimhana), drugs, and a proper diet. The daily use of amalaki, turmeric, and barley, among other natural remedies, may be beneficial. Decoctions of Triphala, Fenugreek, and Shilajit are commonly used in Ayurvedic medicine to treat diabetes.

It is advisable to consult an Ayurvedic doctor for medication tailored to one's specific needs.

Allopathy:

Type 1 Diabetes:

- Insulin (rapid-acting insulin, short-acting insulin, intermediate-acting insulin, and long-acting insulin).

Type 2 Diabetes:

- Alpha-glucosidase inhibitors, biguanides, Dipeptidyl Peptidase-4 (DPP-4) inhibitors, glucagon-like peptides, sodium glucose transport protein 2 (SGLT2) inhibitors, sulfonylureas, and insulin itself.

Additionally, lifestyle modifications such as diet and exercise can be effective in managing blood sugar levels.

Pranayama:

- Abdominal Breathing.
- Viloma Pranayama (3 Levels).
- Bhastrika or Kapalabhati.
- Ujjayi Pranayama.
- Angisara Kriya.

Nutrition for Diabetes:

Diabetes develops due to insufficient insulin production by the pancreas or the body's inability to utilize insulin effectively. Insulin helps regulate glucose levels in the body. The best way to manage diabetes is to lead a healthy lifestyle, maintain a clean diet, and engage in regular physical activity.

A healthy diet includes:

- Replacing saturated fats like cheese, butter, etc. with unsaturated fats like nuts, vegetable oils, etc.
- Cutting down on smoking, excessive drinking, and consuming natural sugars rather than added sugars.
- Including a good amount of dietary fiber from fruits, vegetables, and whole grains.

Consumption of low-GI (glycemic index) foods is also a great way to keep insulin levels in check. Regular physical activity is essential to help keep blood glucose levels under control.

Diets for individuals with diabetes should focus on lowering insulin resistance and promoting weight loss. They should be long-term and sustainable.

Low Carb Diet:

- Carbohydrates have the greatest impact on blood sugar levels as they are broken down into glucose. Therefore, reducing the intake of high amounts of carbohydrates can help manage blood sugar levels.
- Low-carb diets seem to work well in the long term when adhered to. In one study, people with type 2 diabetes ate a low-carb diet for 6 months. Their diabetes remained well managed for more than 3 years if they stuck to the diet. Similarly, when people with type 1 diabetes followed a carb-restricted diet, those who adhered to the diet saw a significant improvement in blood sugar levels over a 4-year period.

Ref: https://www.ncbi.nlm.nih.gov/pmc/articles/PMC2424054/

Food Order or Carbs Last Approach:

Intra-meal timing might also be important for controlling blood glucose levels. Research has shown that starting a meal—breakfast, lunch, and dinner—with protein and fat and consuming carbohydrates at the end of a meal can:

- Reduce postprandial glucose secretion.
- Reduce gastric emptying, which means less glucose entering the blood.
- Enhance glucose-stimulated insulin release.

- Reduce insulin degradation by the liver.

Therefore, having more insulin circulating in the blood leads to a longer duration of blood glucose control.

Ref: https://www.ncbi.nlm.nih.gov/pmc/articles/PMC4876745/

Consumption of Low-GI Food:

The glycemic index (GI) rate of foods is based on the amount of carbohydrates present in each food and how they affect one's blood sugar level when consumed on their own. (It was created in the early 1980s by Dr. David Jenkins, a Canadian professor.) Studies have shown that a low-GI diet may result in weight loss, reduce blood sugar levels, and lower the risk of heart disease and type 2 diabetes.

Consumption of Fiber-Rich Food:

Fiber helps with blood sugar control and weight management. It also reduces the risk of heart disease and keeps the digestive system healthy.

Foods to Consume:

Green Leafy Vegetables	Kale, spinach, arugula, amaranth, fenugreek leaves
Non Starchy Vegetables	Carrots, beans, cabbage, okra, cauliflower, broccoli, asparagus, cucumber with peel, radish, mushrooms, tomatoes, zucchini, ginger, garlic, onions, peas
Fruits	Oranges, avocados, all types of berries, kiwi, guava, papaya, apple, peaches, watermelon, dragon fruit, plums, cherry, pineapple
Protein	Plant Based - Tofu, soya chunks, legumes and lentils like kidney beans, soya beans, pinto beans, moong dal, chana dal, mixed sprouts, unsweetened peanut butter, nuts and seeds like chia seeds, flax seeds, almonds, pistachios, walnuts, hazelnuts Animal Based - Chicken breast, paneer, eggs, greek yogurt, low fat dairy products, fatty fish like salmon, sardines, herring, anchovies, and mackerel are great sources of the omega-3 fatty acids DHA and EPA, which have major benefits for heart health
Grains	Brown rice, black rice, ragi, barley, whole wheat, steel cut oats, quinoa, buckwheat, bulgur

	wheat/daliya, millets, amaranth. Almond flour, chickpea flour/besan are also the best alternative to make rotis.
Sugars	Best sugar alternative is stevia.

Studies show that eating fatty fish may also help regulate blood sugar. A study involving 68 adults who were overweight or obese found that participants who consumed fatty fish had significant improvements in post-meal blood sugar levels compared to participants who consumed lean fish.

Reference: https://pubmed.ncbi.nlm.nih.gov/28606215/

Foods to Avoid:

Starchy Vegetables	Potatoes, corn, butternut squash, sweet potatoes, and canned vegetables
Fruits	Mangoes, bananas, apples, dried and sweetened fruits, canned frozen fruits, fruit juices
Protein	Red meat, high fat dairy products
Grains	White bread, white rice, pasta, maida or any form of refined grains
Sweets	White / brown sugar, honey, fruit jams, spreads which contain a lot of sugar, aerated drinks like sodas, milk, and white chocolates
Others	Alcohol, smoking; Consuming highly processed foods, and fried foods should also be avoided

Clean and healthy eating habits, along with regular physical exercise such as walking, jogging, and yoga, are highly recommended to keep blood sugar levels in control.

LUMBAR ISSUES

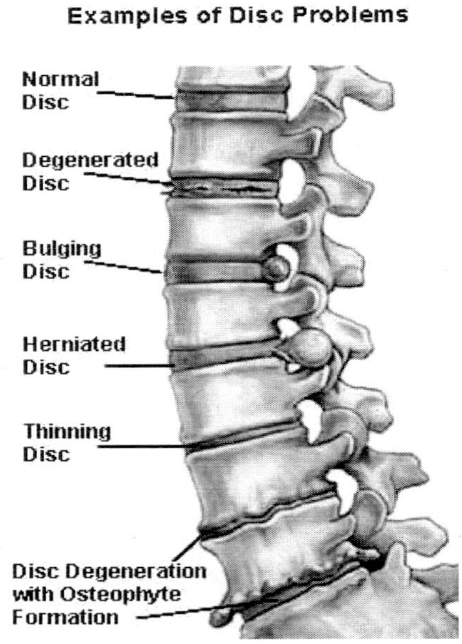

The lumbar region, also called the low back, starts below the ribcage. Every individual experiences pain in the low back at some point in their lifetime. It sometimes improves automatically on its own. However, in some cases, the pain persists for a long period, and in such instances, it is advisable to consult a doctor for better advice and effective treatment.

The lumbar region consists of five individual cylindrical bones that form the spine, composed of vertebral bones, intervertebral discs, nerves, muscles, ligaments, tendons, and blood vessels. Each vertebra on the front side has a large disc acting as a shock absorber, with two cartilage-lined facet joints on its back side. The discs and facet joints function together to provide the spine with the ability to bend and twist safely. Tendons connect muscles to the vertebrae, helping to restrict excessive movement that could harm the spinal cord.

The lower back muscles facilitate a range of movement and stabilize the spine. The spinal column consists of 24 vertebrae stacked on top of each other, with a gel-like structure called a disc between each vertebra providing cushioning. The spinal cord carries nerve signals to and from the brain, forming the central nervous system together with the brain. Ligaments connect two bones, and tendons attach muscles to the bone or another structure.

The important functions of the lower back include:

1. Supporting most of the body weight.

2. Facilitating bending and twisting.
3. Controlling leg movements.

Lower back pain is one of the most common issues people face, primarily caused by mechanical issues and soft-tissue injuries. These injuries include damage to intervertebral discs, compression of nerve roots, and improper movement of spinal joints.

Ayurveda refers to lumbar issues (lower back pain) as "Kati Shoola," where "kati" means "lower back," and "shoola" means "pain." Kati Shoola is mainly caused by the vitiation of Vata dosha. Due to various causative factors, Vata gets vitiated and accumulates in the Kati region, causing back pain. The vitiated Vata residing in the lower back region leads to the absorption of the Sheshalka Kapha (the sub-dosha of Kapha that controls joint lubrication), resulting in reduced joint mobility. This restriction affects the movement of the lumbo-sacral region, including flexion, extension, lateral flexion, and rotation, either completely or partially, depending on the etiological factors.

Causes:

The most common causes of lower back pain are mentioned below:

- **Muscular Problems:** Muscle strain typically occurs due to heavy or incorrect lifting or overstraining the muscles.
- **Degenerated Discs:** Disc degeneration is typically caused by old age and prolonged injuries.
- **Herniated Discs:** Disc herniation can occur slowly as part of natural wear and tear or suddenly due to injury or heavy lifting.
- **Osteoarthritis:** This is an age-related issue where the cartilage covering the facets starts to wear out.
- **Spinal Stenosis:** This occurs due to the narrowing of the spinal canal, which can irritate or press the nerve roots, resulting in sciatica.
- **Tumor:** A new growth in the spine that may spread from existing cancer.
- **Slipped Disc:** An age-related wear and tear where the disks start to dry out.
- **Scoliosis:** A condition where the spine is twisted and out of shape.
- **Kyphosis:** A condition that bends the spine forward.
- **Ankylosing Spondylitis:** A type of arthritis that starts by making the low back and hips rigid and sore, especially early in the morning. As it progresses, it can leave one hunched over.
- **Spinal Cord Injury:** This most often happens due to an accident.

- **Spondylolisthesis:** A condition where the vertebrae slide forward or sideways and don't line up properly.

Symptoms:

Symptoms may vary depending on the pain experienced.

- Pain can be dull or achy, restricted to the lower back area.
- Sciatica pain that starts from the lower back, radiating up to the lower leg or feet.
- Tightness and muscle spasms in the pelvis region.
- Aggravating pain comes with a sedentary lifestyle.
- Difficulty in changing posture.

The pain can be either mechanical or radicular. Other sources of pain can occur due to neuropathic pain, deformity, tumors, infections, pain from inflammation such as rheumatoid arthritis or ankylosing spondylitis, kidney stones, or ulcerative colitis. It is also possible for lower back pain to develop without any specific reason.

Diagnosis:

Diagnosis can be made by doing a physical examination, understanding the pattern of pain, and further by performing x-ray, CT, MRI, EMG, and NCS studies to check for any mechanical or nerve issues.

Yogic Intervention:

Regular practice of yoga is an effective way to manage the symptoms of lower back pain. Studies have shown that stretching and isometric exercises provide great relief for people suffering from lumbar issues. Stretching helps in the maximum elongation of muscle fibers and refines the elasticity of the muscles, whereas isometric posturing strengthens the muscles and relieves muscle spasm and pain. There will be an overall improvement in muscle flexibility, enhanced range of motion, and improved posture with regular practice of yoga.

Case Study:

Subjective: Dr. Sandesh (name changed), a dentist, had long-standing severe back pain and had not been managing his pain for a long time, though he was taking pain relief medications prescribed by a neurologist.

Objective: Dr. Sandesh had numerous medical tests only to find out that his condition had aggravated due to the poor posture he maintained at work.

Assessment: Though he could manage his pain with medications, he just wanted to have a permanent solution for this problem. The neurologist advised him to take up a physical exercise routine, and he came to our center.

Plan: Assessing his body movements, we designed a yoga regimen (20 sessions) using props, which helped him attain strength and flexibility.

Now, Mr. Sandesh is a regular yoga practitioner and visits us from time to time for any corrections in his yoga practice.

- **Surya Namaskar (Sun Salutations):**

A modified version of Surya Namaskar can be performed under the guidance of a therapeutic yoga teacher.

- **Asanas (Yoga Postures):**

The following are some postures that are helpful in managing the symptoms of low back pain.

1. Samakonasana (Equal / Right Angle Pose):

Steps To Perform:

1. Stand in Tadasana, spread the feet trunk width apart.
2. Inhale, lengthen the torso, exhale, fold forward from the trunk and bring the chest parallel to the floor, maintain the length in the spine, extend both the arms straight in front, shoulder width apart.
3. Stay and breathe here for 30 seconds to 1 minute.
4. Inhale and come back to Tadasana.

Joint Actions:

- Anterior pelvic tilt with forward lumbar spine flexion.
- Thoracic and cervical spine in neutral.
- Complete flexion of shoulders with extension of elbows, forearms mid prone with wrists in neutral.
- Knee extension with ankle in neutral position.

Main Muscle Actions:

- Contraction of erector spinae muscles.
- Contraction of deltoid muscles.
- Stretching of hamstring and gastrocnemius muscles.

Things To Focus On:

- Activate the quads and spread the body weight equally on all four edges on the feet.

- Pull the knee caps, engage the shoulders as you stretch the arms forward and reach the tips of the fingers forward.
- Engage the core muscles, lengthen the torso without straining the neck.

Things To Be Cared For:

- People with joint, back, neck pain should practice this pose under the supervision of a therapeutic yoga teacher.

Samakonasana Variation 1

Samakonasana Variation 2

2. Prasarita Padottanasana (Wide Legged Forward Fold):

Steps To Perform:

1. Spread the feet 4 to 5 feet with the toes pointing in slightly.
2. Inhale, lengthen the torso, exhale, fold forward from the trunk bringing the chest parallel to the floor, rest the palms on the mat right under the shoulders.
3. Inhale, look up, lengthen the torso again, exhale, fold forward and reach the crown of the head in between the palms.
4. Stay and breathe here for 30 seconds to 1 minute.
5. Inhale and come out of the pose.

Joint Actions:

- Forward flexion of the lumbar spine.
- Abduction and anterior pelvic tilt.
- Knee extension and ankle in neutral position.
- Slight Flexion and abduction of the shoulder with elbow flexion.
- Forearm pronation with wrist extension.

Main Muscle Actions:

- Stretches the hip adductor group muscles.
- Contraction of rectus and transversus abdominis muscles.
- Contraction of deltoid and biceps brachii muscles.

Things To Focus On:

- Focus on activating the quads, hip flexors and engage the feet by pressing the inner and outer edges completely on the mat.
- Engage the glutes by squeezing, core muscles by tucking the tailbone, focus on lengthening the torso and keep the spine long.
- Focus on pushing the buttocks back and trunk forward, activating the muscles around the inner thighs, fold forward, and stretch the back of the legs, keeping the shoulders and neck relaxed.

Things To Be Cared For:

- People with recent or chronic injury to the legs, hips, ankles, back, shoulders, recovering from surgery of any internal organs should avoid this pose.
- People with high blood pressure, migraine, arthritis of the knees, hips, or shoulders or those with fibromyalgia should practice this under the supervision of a therapeutic yoga teacher.

Prasarita Paddotanasana Variation 1

Prasarita Paddotanasana Variation 2

3. Sarala Bhujangasana (Easy Cobra Pose):

Steps To Perform:

1. Lie on the stomach in Makarasana.
2. Rest the forearms on the mat, shoulders are stacked above the elbows.
3. Inhale, push the chest away from the floor, gently arch the back.
4. Stay and breathe for 30 seconds to 1 minute.
5. Exhale, come back to Makarasana.

Joint Actions:

- Extension of the spine.
- Shoulder in abduction with elbow flexion, forearm pronation and wrists in neutral.
- Internal rotation of the hip.
- Plantarflexion of the ankle.

Main Muscle Actions:

- Contraction of erector spinae muscles and gluteal muscle.
- Stretches the rectus and transversus abdominis muscle.
- Contraction of shoulder retractor muscles.

Things To Focus On:

- Focus on activating the lower limbs, squeeze the glutes, thighs, point the toes back.

- Keep the forearms shoulder width apart, activate the core muscles, push the shoulders down and away from the ears, engage the tips of the fingers, rest the pelvis on the floor, keep neck neutral and gaze straight ahead without straining the neck.

Things To Be Cared For:

- People suffering from hernia, peptic ulcer, hyperthyroidism or intestinal tuberculosis should practice this pose under the supervision of a therapeutic yoga teacher.
- Women should avoid this pose during pregnancy and menstrual cycle.

4. Shashankasana (Moon Pose / Hare Or Rabbit Pose):

Steps To Perform:

1. Sit in Vajrasana.
2. Inhale, lengthen the torso, exhale, fold forward from the trunk stretching the lower back and try to reach the forehead on the mat.
3. Stay and breathe for 30 seconds to 1 minute.
4. Inhale and come back to Vajrasana.

Joint Actions:

- Flexion of hip and knee with ankle plantar flexion.
- Flexion of lumbosacral spine.
- Flexion of shoulder and extension of elbow with pronation of forearm.

Main Muscle Actions:

- Contraction of rectus and transversus abdominis muscles.
- Contraction of hamstring and gastrocnemius muscles.
- Stretching of latissimus dorsi and intercostal muscles.

Things To Focus On:

- Focus on lengthening the torso, internally rotating the hips to keep the knees together. Only if you find it difficult to breathe in the final position with the knees together, widen the knees and create some space to breathe.
- Walk the hands forward and engage the shoulders, reaching the finger tips forward, stretch on the obliques.
- Keep the buttocks on the heels.

Things To Be Cared For:

- Practice this pose under the supervision of a therapeutic yoga teacher if you have high blood pressure, glaucoma, dizziness, vertigo, knee issues, slip disc, hernia, shoulder issue, neck issue.
- Women should avoid this asana during pregnancy.

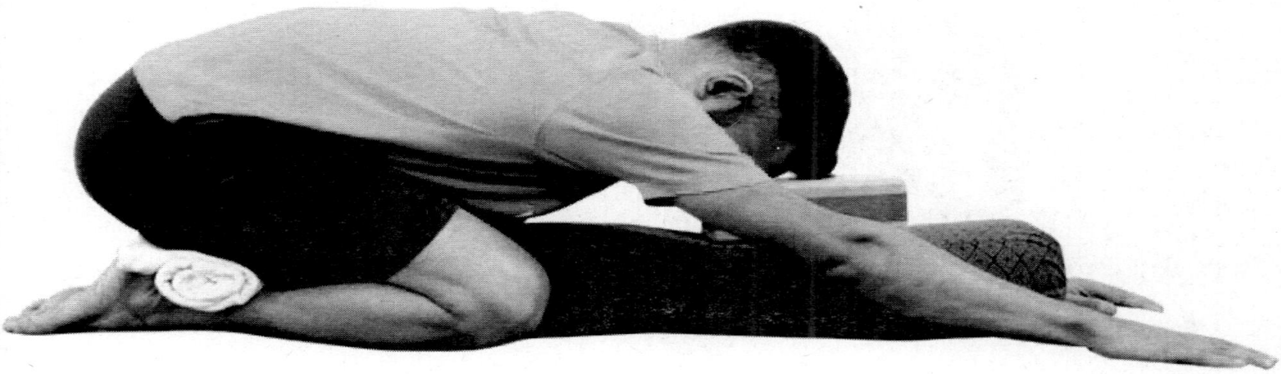

Shashankasana Variation 1

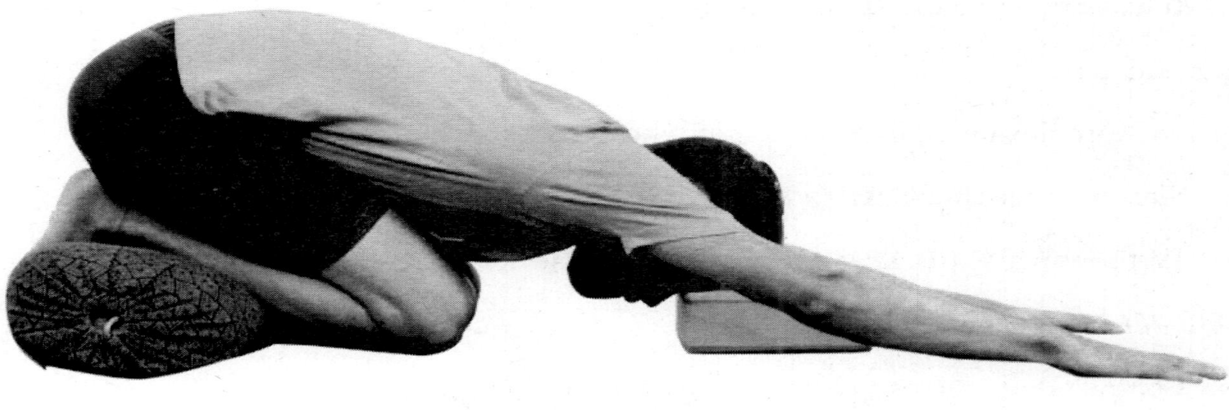

Shashankasana Variation 2

5. Urdhva Mukha Paschimottanasana (Upward Facing Seated Forward Bend):

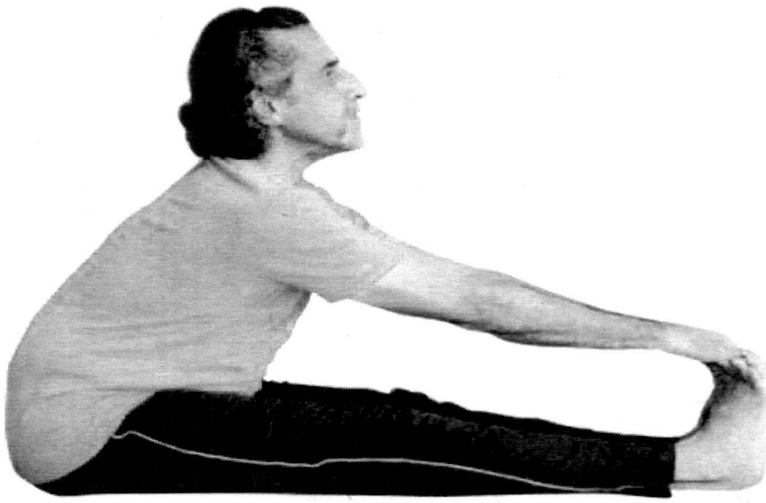

Steps To Perform:

1. Sit in Dandasana with your feet together.
2. Inhale, lengthen the torso, exhale, bend forward from the trunk, try to grasp the feet and flex the toes in, keep the spine long, head and chin up.
3. Stay and breathe here for 30 seconds to 1 minute.
4. Inhale and come back to Dandasana.

Joint Actions:

- ➢ Forward flexion of the lumbar spine and slight extension of the cervical spine.
- ➢ Flexion of the shoulders, extension of the elbows and pronation of the forearms.
- ➢ Posterior pelvic tilt, knee extension with ankle dorsiflexion.

Main Muscle Actions:

- ➢ Contraction of rectus and transversus abdominis muscles.
- ➢ Stretching of gluteus, hamstring and gastrocnemius muscles.

Things To Focus On:

- ➢ Engage the thighs and draw the legs closer to each other pressing them on the floor, flex the toes towards the shin bone to stretch the calves and hamstrings.
- ➢ Activate the core muscles as you bend forward, lengthen the torso and stretch the back.

Things To Be Cared For:

- Perform this pose under the supervision of a therapeutic yoga teacher if you are suffering from asthma, dysentery, recent back injury, injury to your arms, hips, ankles or are pregnant.

Urdhva Mukha Paschimottanasana
Variation 1

Urdhva Mukha Paschimottanasana Variation 2

6. Urdhva Mukha Upavistha Konasana (Upward Facing Seated Wide Legged Forward Bend)

Steps To Perform:

1. Sit in Dandasana with both feet together.
2. Fold the knees, grasp the big toes, raise the heels above the ground and spread the legs wide apart.
3. Inhale, lengthen the torso, open the chest, look straight ahead.
4. Stay and breathe for 30 seconds to 1 minute.
5. Inhale and come back to Dandasana.

Joint Actions:

- Forward flexion of lumbar spine.
- Anterior pelvic tilt of hips.
- Abduction of the shoulders and extension of the elbows.
- Abduction and external rotation of the hips.

Main Muscle Actions:

- Stretching of hip adductor muscles.
- Stretching of gastrocnemius muscles.
- Flexion of hip flexor muscle group.
- Contraction of quadriceps femoris muscles.
- Contraction of neck extensor muscle group.

Things To Focus On:

- Activate the quads, abductor muscles and roll the thighs in such that the thighs are facing the ceiling and stretch the groin, back of the knees and hamstrings.
- Keep the spine long, shoulders and neck relaxed.

Things To Be Cared For:

- Practice this pose under the supervision of a therapeutic yoga teacher if you are pregnant, suffering from herniated disc, injuries on lower-back, hamstring, groin, hips & knees.

Urdhva Mukha Upavishta Konasana Variation 1

Urdhva Mukha Upavishta Konasana Variation 2

7. Urdhva Prasarita Eka Padasana (Supine Single Leg Raised Pose):

Steps To Perform:

1. Lie on the back with legs extended, feet together and your arms alongside the body, palms facing down for the support.
2. Inhale, lift the right leg up 90 degrees.
3. Stay and breathe here for 30 seconds to 1 minute.
4. Exhale and gently bring the right leg down.
5. Repeat the same on the side leg.

Joint Actions:

- Neutral spine.
- Flexion of hip with extension of knee and dorsiflexion of ankle of the upper leg.
- Neutral position of hip with knee extension of the lower leg.

Main Muscle Actions:

- Iliacus, psoas major, rectus femoris muscle contraction.
- Stretching of gastrocnemius muscles.

Things To Focus On:

- Keep your core engaged by drawing your navel in as you lift the leg up and without allowing your belly to pop up.

- Keep the neck relaxed and neutral and press the palms firmly on the mat as you lift the leg up for support.

Things To Be Cared For:

- People suffering from high blood pressure, slipped discs should avoid this asana or practice under the supervision of a therapeutic yoga teacher.
- People suffering from ulcer or have undergone recent abdominal surgery should avoid this asana.

Urdhva Prasarita Ek Padasana Variation 1

Urdhva Prasarita Ek Padasana Variation 2

8. Dwi Pada Pithasana (Two Legged Table Pose):

Steps To Perform:

1. Lie on the back, bend the knees and keep the feet trunk width apart, heels closer to the buttocks.
2. Inhale, squeeze the glutes, lift the hips above the ground arching the spine, feel the weight on the shoulders and arms.
3. Stay and breathe for 30 seconds to 1 minute.
4. Exhale and release.

Joint Actions:

- Extension of both lower thoracic and lumbar spine.
- Flexion of upper thoracic spine.
- Retraction of scapula.
- Shoulder in neutral with elbow extension.
- Forearm in mid prone position and wrist in neutral position.
- Hip extension with knee flexion and ankle in neutral position.

Main Muscle Actions:

- Contraction of gluteal muscle and hamstring muscles.
- Contraction of shoulder retractor group muscles.

Things To Focus On:

- Focus on internally rotating the hips by engaging the hip flexors, adductor muscles of the thighs, draw the knees in, and point the toes forward.

- Engage the shoulders by pushing them on the mat, squeeze the glutes and activate the lower back muscles.
- Keep the neck and shoulder relaxed.

Things To Be Cared For:

- Avoid this pose if you have migraine, neck issues, breathing issues like flu, bronchitis, throat infections, have weak stomach, intestine, have undergone knee replacement surgery, have osteoporosis. Else, should practice this under the supervision of a therapeutic yoga teacher.
- Women should avoid this pose during pregnancy, since it puts pressure in the lower abdomen and the internal organs thus making breathing difficult which can be harmful for the fetus.

Dwipada Peethasana Variation 1

Dwipada Peethasana Variation 2

9. Jathara Parivartanasana (Revolved Abdomen Pose):

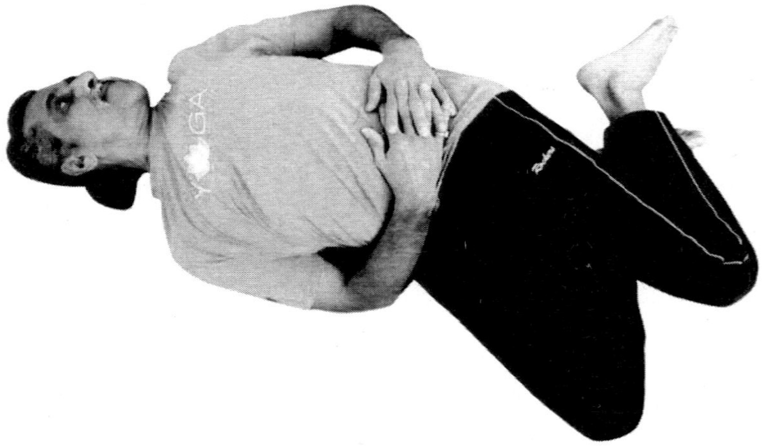

Steps To Perform:

1. Lie on the back, bend the knees keeping the feet trunk width apart with the palms on the belly.
2. Exhale, drop both the knees to the right side, twisting the spine, turn the head in the opposite direction.
3. Bring the left shoulder to the floor, open the chest.
4. Stay and breathe here for 30 seconds to 1 minute.
5. Inhale, come out of the pose and repeat on the other side.

Joint Actions:

- Lateral rotation of the cervical spine.
- Rotation of the lower lumbar spine.
- Extension, internal rotation and adduction of the left hip when moving to the right side.
- Flexion, external rotation and abduction of the right hip when moving to the right side.
- Flexion of the knees with the ankle in neutral position.

Main Muscle Actions:

- Contraction of scalene, splenius capitis and sternocleidomastoid muscles of the neck.
- Stretching of quadratus lumborum and external oblique muscles.
- Contraction of hamstring and tibialis anterior muscle.

- Stretches the hip flexors muscle group.

Things To Focus On:

- Focus on reaching the shoulders on the mat and expand the ribcage.
- Engage the hip flexors as you drop the knees sideways to stretch muscles around the hips and lower back.

Things To Be Cared For:

- Avoid practicing this pose if you have a herniated disc, injury of the hips, spine, shoulders, neck, rib cage or have fibromyalgia or any bone related issues.
- Women during pregnancy or post pregnancy or people having issues with the back, knee, ankle, arthritis of the hips should practice this under the supervision of a therapeutic yoga teacher.

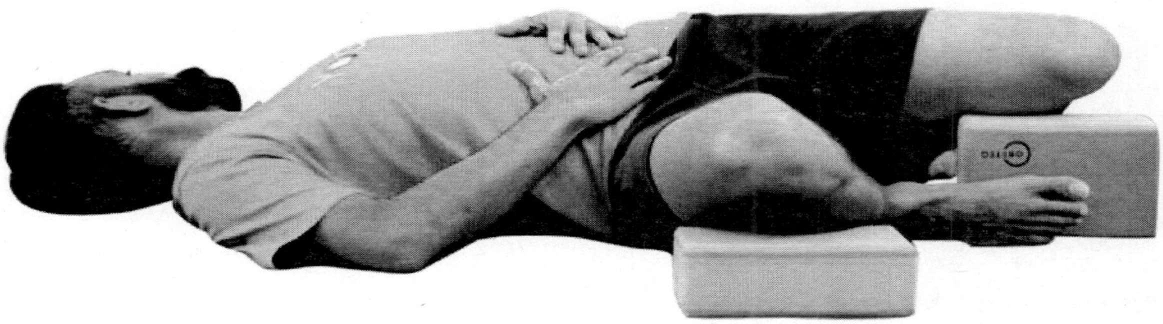

Jatara Parivrittasana Variation 1

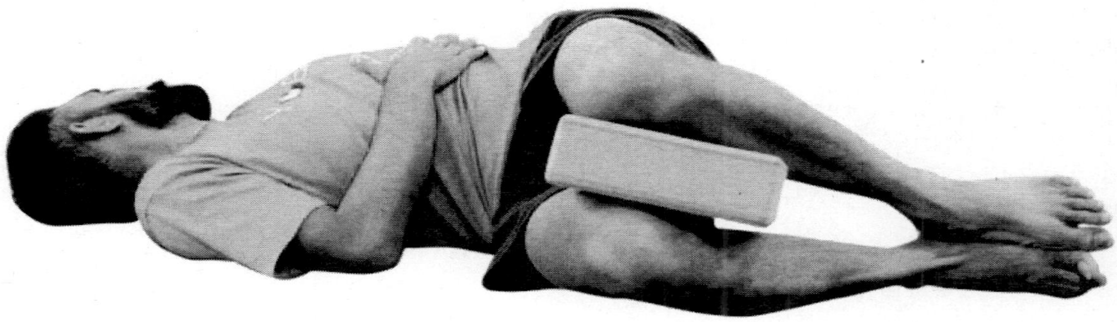

Jatara Parivrittasana Variation 2

Treatment for Lumbar Issues:

Ayurveda: Some of the ayurvedic treatment includes:

- Snehana (Oleation Therapy).
- Swedana (Steam treatment).
- Virechana.
- Therapies like Abhyanga (Massage with medicated oil), Kati Basti (Oil pooling in the Lumbosacral region), Upanaha (Applying herbal pastes), Virechana (Therapeutic Purgation), Baspha Sweda (Steam, often after Abhyanga), Basti (Medicated Enemas), Patra Pinda Sweda (Medicated fomentation through pain relieving herbs).
- Lifestyle modifications – clean diet, yoga, exercise (vyayama).
- Ayurvedic treatments are based on the ayurvedic diagnosis. Hence, consult an ayurvedic doctor for proper medication.

Allopathy:

- Muscle relaxants.
- Narcotic pain medications.
- Back/Neck braces.
- Epidural steroid injections.

Pranayama:

- Abdominal breathing.
- Viloma pranayama (3 levels).
- Ujjayi pranayama.
- Nadi shodhana.
- Bhramari.

Other than these, it can be controlled by making some lifestyle changes. Some non-medical treatments include:

- Manual manipulation.
- Acupuncture.
- Massage therapy.
- Mindful meditation.

Nutrition For Lumbar Issues:

Lower back pain can be minor or major which can be caused due to long hours of sitting, standing, walking or weakness of the muscles and joints. Minor lower back pain can be treated by strengthening the back muscles through exercise. But when the pain reaches a point where it gets challenging to even walk from one place to another, one is advised to rest during the initial stage of injury.

Diet plays an important role here, because while resting it's easy to put on a few kilos, which can adversely affect the situation.

Foods to Consume:

It is important to get all the needed vitamins and minerals like calcium, iron, vitamin D, magnesium, vitamin C, vitamin B12, and proteins. Fiber-rich foods will keep one feeling fuller for longer.

Anti-Inflammatory Food	Fresh fruits and vegetables, green leafy vegetables, nuts and seeds
Easily Digestible Foods	Food that is light on the stomach - warm vegetable soup, salads, rice and dal, khichdi
Whole Grains	Ragi, wheat, barley, oats, brown rice, red rice
Food Rich in Calcium & Vitamin D	Milk and milk products like paneer, cheese, spinach, soybean
Protein	Soya chunks, quinoa, sprouts, dal, flax seeds and chia seeds, eggs

Foods to Avoid:

- Calorie Dense Food - food that triggers intolerance causing bloating or any form of irritation in the digestive tract
- Processed / Packaged Food - like white bread , chips, biscuits, ready to eat food items
- Oily and Fatty Food
- Fatty meat

It is best to follow a vegetarian/plant based/sattvic diet if one is suffering from lumbar issues. Food gives us energy and helps heal / recover faster when there is proper consumption of all the vitamins and minerals that our body needs.

ARTHRITIS

Rheumatoid Arthritis in Hand

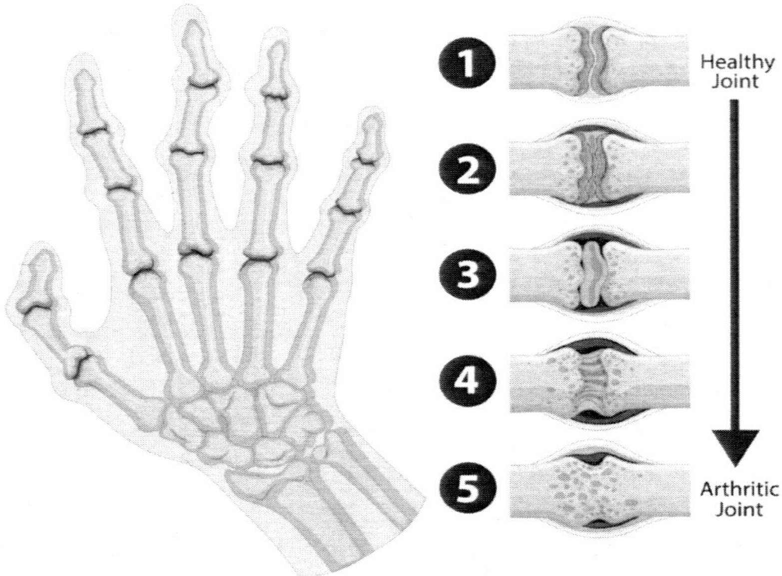

Arthritis is a disease that causes inflammation or degradation of the joints in the body. The joints in the body are those areas where two bones are connected. Arthritis affects the joints, causing swelling and pain, which is further referred to as arthralgia.

In some cases, the condition can cause damage to the skin, blood vessels, lungs, and heart. It is even referred to as an autoimmune disease.

They are classified into:

- **Monoarthritis:** When only a single joint is involved.
- **Oligoarthritis:** When two or three joints are involved.
- **Polyarthritis:** When four or more joints are involved.

It is most common among women and occurs more frequently as people get older, limiting everyday activities that involve the movement of the joints.

The reason for detecting more of this arthritis in women is exclusively for their tendons, which work like a lever to provide childbirth, being more elastic and susceptible to injuries.

There are over 100 kinds of arthritis, and the most familiar ones are:

- **Rheumatoid Arthritis:** This is a chronic inflammatory disease that disrupts many joints, including hands and feet. In this condition, the immune system attacks its tissue, and in acute cases, it strikes the internal organs as well.
- **Osteoarthritis:** This is a kind of arthritis that can happen when the supple tissue in the joints of the bone starts to degenerate.
- **Psoriatic Arthritis:** This is a kind of arthritis affecting those people who have a skin disease called psoriasis. There is no cure for this disease.
- **Reactive Arthritis:** This condition is an inflammatory arthritis affecting major joints like the knees and ankles. It can affect the joints after an infection in some parts of the body. The duration of suffering in this condition will be from 6 months to several years or lifelong, depending upon the severity of the affected areas and the age.
- **Ankylosing Spondylitis:** This condition is also an inflammatory disease that starts to degenerate the spine and major joints. This condition can be seen mostly among men early in their adulthood.
- **Gout:** In this form of arthritis, people suffer severe pain, redness, and stiffness occurring in the joints. The deposit of a huge amount of uric acid in the joints causes pain and inflammation.
- **Juvenile Arthritis:** It is most commonly detected in children under 16 years. It can cause continuous joint pain, stiffness, and swelling in the affected areas. It can last for a few months in some children, while in others, it can last longer.

According to Ayurveda, when unhealthy doshas accumulate in the tissues and damage them, diseases can manifest in physical, accidental, or psychic ways. If the issue is related to the mind or the body, they have a direct impact on each other. That is, if one has a physical disorder, it will affect the mind in the long run.

Joint disorders can occur due to an imbalance in one or a combination of the doshas or even obstruction from one dosha or dhatu (element) to the others. Vata-afflicted joints can cause conditions like osteoarthritis, gout, and fibromyalgia. Pitta-afflicted joints can cause rheumatoid arthritis (amavata), gout, and inflammatory diseases. Both doshas combined can produce degeneration of the articular tissues. Joint issues can also start manifesting at the mental level, which are classified as Manasika Roga (psychological issues). Here are some manifestations at the mental level that can affect the physical level: stress, depression, and insomnia.

Causes:

- Degeneration of the cartilage in the joints.
- **Arthritis in the Family:** Some types of arthritis are seen in families, which can affect family members if parents or siblings carry a particular kind of arthritis.

- **Age:** With advancing age, there is a risk of developing many types of arthritis, mainly osteoarthritis, rheumatoid arthritis, or gout.
- **Injury:** Those who have had an injury to the joint in the past are susceptible to developing arthritis in that joint.
- **Obesity**: Those who are obese have the highest percentage of developing arthritis in the knees, hips, or spine.
- **Medications:** With prolonged use of medicines, the joints can start to degenerate, causing arthritis.
- **Calcium:** Consumption of low-calcium-rich foods can cause arthritis.
- **Smoking:** Smoking is a cause of arthritis.
- **Alcohol**: Consumption of alcohol in excessive amounts can also degenerate the joints, leading to arthritis.

Symptoms:

- Pain in the joints, ankles, fingers, hands, back, neck, or wrists.
- Pain can be sporadic or severe.
- Pain can be muscular, affecting the normal range of motion, making it difficult to walk, or causing weakness in the muscles.
- Stiffness is noticed in the joints, as is swelling.
- Fatigue.
- Bony lumps form in the fingers or toes in the form of bone spurs.
- Deformity, mainly in the toes and fingers, redness, or stiffness in the neck.

Diagnosis:

- Physical examination and medical history of the patient.
- Blood tests: CBC, erythrocyte sedimentation rate (ESR), rheumatoid factor (RF), antinuclear antibodies (ANAs).
- X-rays.
- Arthroscopy, MRI, and CT scan.

Yogic Intervention:

Regular practice of yoga is an effective way to manage the symptoms of arthritis. Studies have shown that stretching, isometric exercises, posture alignment, strengthening of muscles, endurance, and balancing provide great relief for people suffering from arthritis. Stretching refines the muscle's elasticity, whereas isometric posturing strengthens the muscles, joints, and ligaments, helping to ease the pain and stiffness. The asanas are targeted to improve range of motion and posture.

Case Study:

Subjective: Shilpa (name changed) a 15-year-old student who was suffering from severe stiffness and pain in the joints, was brought to our yoga center by her parents seeking relief through yoga.

Objective: We counseled the parents, told them that she has symptoms of arthritis, and asked them to take up an orthopedic consultation.

Assessment: Upon investigation, Seema was diagnosed with arthritis. She was advised to take up regular exercise and was prescribed medications.

Plan: The parents were very happy with the guidance and joined her for yoga therapy (10 sessions) immediately.

Seema has been doing well in her academics for the past two years and has been coping with her arthritis with minimum medication and regular practice of therapeutic yoga (designed for her arthritis).

- **Surya Namaskar (Sun Salutation):**

A modified version of Surya Namaskar can be practiced under the guidance of a therapeutic yoga teacher.

- **Asanas (Yoga Postures):**

The following are some postures that are helpful in managing arthritis.

1. Tadasana in Paschima Baddha Hasta (Mountain Pose With Bound Hands Behind the Back):

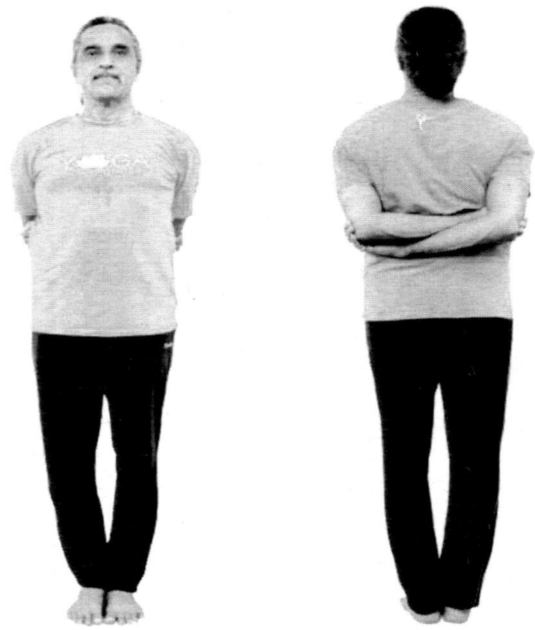

Steps To Perform:

1. Stand in Tadasana.
2. Spread the legs trunk-width apart.
3. Inhale, lengthen the spine, roll the shoulders back, bend the elbows, and grasp the elbows with opposite hands behind the back.
4. Stay and breathe here for 30 seconds to 1 minute.
5. Exhale, release the arms, and come back to Tadasana.

Joint Actions:

- Neutral position of the spine.
- Shoulder extension with elbow flexion.
- Forearm supination with wrist flexion.
- Neutral position of the hip.
- Extension of the knee with a neutral position of the foot.

Main Muscle Actions:

- Retractors and the extensor muscle group of the shoulders.

- Elbow flexor muscles.
- Erector spinae muscles.

Things To Focus On:

- Maintain the alignment of Tadasana throughout the pose.
- Keep the shoulders over the hips and the hips in line with the ankles.
- Engage the large muscles in the thighs, giving the body a stable base.

Things To Be Cared For:

- People with headaches, insomnia, exhaustion, or low blood pressure should avoid this asana.
- People with neck or shoulder pain should practice this under the supervision of a therapeutic yoga teacher.
- Pregnant women should widen their stances as much as necessary to feel stable.

2. Ardha Garudasana (Half-Eagle Pose):

Steps To Perform:

1. Stand in Tadasana and bring the arms forward while keeping them parallel to the floor; cross the right arm over the left arm; and bend the elbows so that the arms are perpendicular to the floor.
2. Slowly turn the hands with the palms facing each other, press the palms against each other, and stretch the fingers upwards.
3. Keep the gaze focused.
4. Stay and breathe here for 30 seconds to 1 minute.
5. Exhale, come out of the pose, and repeat on the other side.

Joint Actions:

- Neutral position of the spine.
- Adduction and flexion of the shoulder at 90 degrees.
- Flexion of elbows.
- Pronation of the forearm with the wrist in a neutral position.

Main Muscle Actions:

- Contraction of pectoralis muscles.
- Elbow flexors and pronation of muscles.

Things To Focus On:

- Engage the shoulder blades by moving them away from each other and lifting them up; interlock the hands while engaging the upper arms; and ensure that the backs of the hands are facing each other.
- Distribute the body weight on both feet equally to maintain balance.

Things To Be Cared For:

- This asana must be avoided if there is a serious wrist or shoulder injury.

Ardha Garudasana
Variation 1

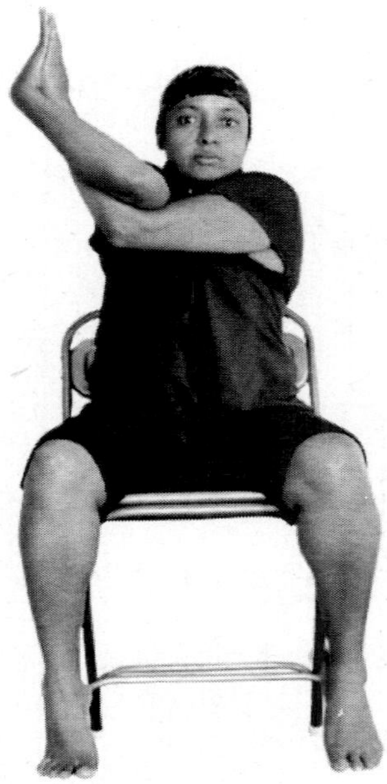

Ardha Garudasana
Variation 2

3. Dwi Pada Prasaranasana (High Plank Pose):

Steps To Perform:

1. Sit in vajrasana.
2. Bend forward by extending the arms in front and placing the palms on the mat, shoulder-width apart.
3. By pressing the palms down on the mat, raise the knees above the ground, coming on the toes, and keeping the body slant from head to heels.
4. Stay and breathe here for 30 seconds to 1 minute.
5. Exhale and come back to Vajrasana.

Joint Actions:

- Neutral position of the spine.
- Flexion of the shoulders to 90 degrees with elbow extension.
- Pronation of the forearm with a wrist extension.
- Hip in a neutral position.
- knee extension with a neutral position of the foot.

Main Muscle Actions:

- Contraction of the rectus and transversus abdominis muscles.
- Flexor group of shoulder muscles.
- Contraction of quadriceps femoris muscles.
- Contraction lumbar extensor group of muscles.
- Contraction of wrist extensor muscles.

Things To Focus On:

- Keep the shoulders stacked right on top of the wrist, and keep the elbows straight. Engage the fingers, palms, and wrists by spreading the fingers wide and pressing the fingers and palms on the mat.
- Keep lifting the shoulder blades up and away from each other.
- Draw the navel in, tuck the tailbone back to engage the core, engage the thigh muscles, and keep pushing the floor away with the palms of the hands. Feel like pressing the heels back against a wall. Engage the legs by pressing them against each other without moving the legs to feel the core working.
- Keep the neck and jaws relaxed, and look at the floor slightly in front of the palms.
- Do not drop the hips or lift them higher than the line of the body.

Things To Be Cared For:

- This asana must be avoided if there is a serious wrist injury or carpal tunnel syndrome.

Dwipada Prasaranasana Variation 1

4. Urdhva Mukha Svanasana (Upward Facing Dog):

Steps To Perform:

1. Lie on the belly, feet hip-width apart, toes pointing back. Place the palms right below the shoulders by the sides of the chest.
2. Inhale, press the palms, and push the chest away from the floor, arching the back. Keep the knees and thighs off the floor.
3. Stay here and breathe for 30 seconds to 1 minute.
4. Exhale and come out of the pose.

Joint Actions:

- Extension of the spine.
- Extension of the hip with mild flexion of the knee and plantar flexion of the ankle.
- Mild flexion of the shoulder, extension of the elbows, and wrist extension.

Main Muscle Actions:

- Contraction of the erector spinae muscles and gluteal muscle group.
- Stretching of the iliacus, quadriceps femoris, rectus, and transversus abdominis muscles.

Things To Focus On:

- Activate the glutes, quads, and toes to engage the lower limbs; focus on keeping the knees and thighs off the floor as you arch the back and look up towards the ceiling.
- Draw the navel in and engage the core to feel the stretch in the abdomen.

- Engage the shoulder blades by rolling them back and down. Try to bring the scapula closer to each other, pushing the chest forward to expand the ribs and create space to breathe.
- Keep the neck neutral.

Things To Be Cared For:

- People suffering from a hernia, back injuries, headaches, or those who have undergone recent abdominal surgeries, pregnant women, or women in their menstrual cycle should avoid practicing this pose.
- People with lower back, neck, knee, ankle, and shoulder pain should practice this under the supervision of a therapeutic yoga teacher.

Urdhva Mukha Shvanasana Variation 1

Urdhva Mukha Shvanasana Variation 2

5. Ardha Pincha Mayurasana (Half-Feathered Peacock Pose):

Steps To Perform:

1. Sit in vajrasana.
2. Place the forearms on the mat shoulder-width apart by extending the body forward.
3. Come on the toes and lift the knees off the floor, coming to an inverted V.
4. Stay and breathe here for 30 seconds to 1 minute.
5. Come back to Vajrasana.

Joint Actions:

- Lumbar flexion of the spine.
- 120-degree flexion and slight abduction of the shoulder joint.
- Flexion of the elbows with pronation of the forearms.
- Stand in a neutral position.
- Anterior pelvic tilt of the hip with mild hip flexion.
- Extension of the knees.
- Dorsiflexion of the ankles.

Main Muscle Actions:

- Flexor group of hip muscles.
- Shoulder and elbow flexor groups of muscles.
- Stretching of the hamstring and gastrocnemius muscles.

Things To Focus On:

- Focus on engaging the forearms, fingers, and palms by pressing them onto the floor.

- Engage the shoulder blades by pushing them away from each other and lifting them upward.
- Engage the hip flexors and the shoulders to lengthen the spine, reaching up high through the tailbone.
- Focus on keeping the feet hip-width apart with the toes facing forward; press the heels into the floor to feel a stretch in the back of the legs.

Things To Be Cared For:

- People suffering from recent or recurring shoulder, back, arm, or neck injuries should avoid practicing this pose.
- People suffering from high blood pressure should practice this pose under the supervision of a therapeutic yoga teacher.

Ardha Pincha Mayurasana Variation 1

Ardha Pincha Mayurasana Variation 2

6. Uttana Pristhasana (Lizard Pose):

Steps To Perform:

1. Come to Adho Mukha Svanasana, inhale, bring the right leg forward, and place the sole of the right foot outside the right palm.
2. Exhale, sink the hips, stretch the left leg back, come on the left toes, and keep the left knee up.
3. Stay and breathe here for 30 seconds to 1 minute.
4. Exhale, come back to Adho Mukha Svanasana, and repeat on the other side.

Joint Actions:

- Neutral position of the spine.
- Shoulder flexion with elbow extension.
- Forearm pronation with wrist extension.

- Extension of the hip and mild flexion of the knee with the ankle in a neutral position of the extended leg.
- Flexion of the hip and 90 degrees of knee with the neutral position of the ankle of the bent leg.
- Cervical in a neutral position.

Main Muscle Actions:

- Flexor muscle group of hip and knee at the bent leg.
- Extensor muscles of the hip at the extended leg.
- Stretching of hip flexor group muscles at the extended leg.
- The shoulder flexor group of muscles and the elbow and wrist extensor groups of muscles.

Things To Focus On:

- Focus on engaging the sole of the bent knee and the toes of the extended knee to form a stable base, and keep pushing the heel of the extended leg backward.
- Engage the shoulder blades by pushing them away from each other, and focus on engaging the spinal extensors to maintain the length of the spine.
- Engage the hip flexors and extensors to feel the stretch on the hips and quads.

Things To Be Cared For:

- People suffering from hip, neck, knee, shoulder, back, or spine injuries and with recent abdominal, brain, or heart surgeries should practice this asana under a therapeutic yoga teacher.

Uttana Prishtasana Variation 1

Uttana Prishtasana Variation 2

7. Makarasana (Crocodile Pose):

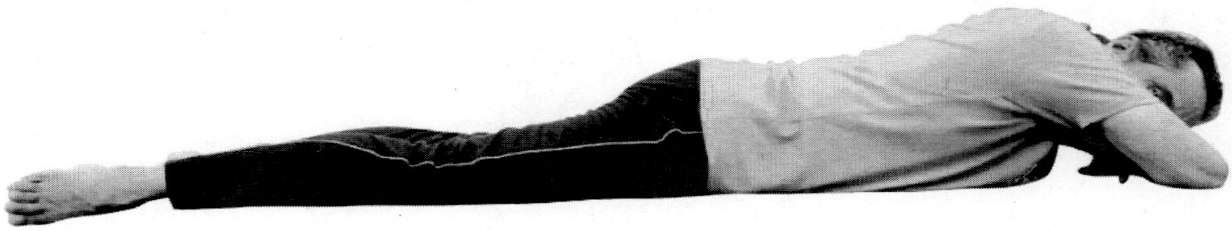

Steps To Perform:

1. Lie on the belly, with the legs spread mat width apart, toes pointing out, bend the elbows, point them sideways, and rest one palm on top of the other.

2. Rest the cheek on the palms.

3. Stay and breathe here for 30 seconds to 5 minutes.

Joint Actions:

- Neutral position of the spine.
- Retraction of the scapula.
- Flexion of the bilateral elbow, shoulders 90 degrees abduction.
- Abduction and internal rotation of the hip.
- Extension of the knee.
- Eversion of ankles.

Main Muscle Actions:

- Erector spinae muscles.
- Middle fibers of deltoid muscles.

Things To Focus On:

- Focus on normal inhalation and exhalation without forcing the breath in any way, relaxing the entire body.

Things To Be Cared For:

- People with back and neck injuries and deep psychological issues should practice this asana only under the supervision of a therapeutic yoga teacher.

8. Urdhva Mukha Janu Sirsasana (Upward Facing Head to Knee Pose):

Steps To Perform:

1. Sit in Dandasana.
2. Bend the left knee, place the sole of the left foot against the right inner thigh, and heel close to the perineum.
3. Inhale, raise the arms, and lengthen the spine.
4. Exhale, fold forward, and grasp the right foot with both hands.
5. With a further exhalation, keep pushing the trunk forward without rounding the back, and keep the head up.
6. Stay and breathe here for 30 seconds to 1 minute.
7. Inhale, come out of the pose, and repeat on the other side.

Joint Actions:

- Lumbar flexion of the spine.
- Cervical extension.
- Flexion of shoulders and extension of elbows.
- Mild prone position of forearm with wrist extension.
- Hip in a neutral position, extension of knee with dorsiflexion of the ankle of the extended leg.
- Flexion, abduction, and external rotation of the hip at the folded leg.
- Knee flexion with ankle plantar flexion of the folded leg.

Main Muscle Actions:

- Stretching of the hamstring and gastrocnemius muscles.
- Contraction of the hip flexors and abductor muscle groups.
- Contraction of the shoulder flexor muscle group.

Things To Focus On:

- Focus on internally rotating the outstretched leg, engage the hip flexors, and press the sole of the opposite foot against the inner thigh.
- Engage the core muscles by tucking the tailbone in as one folds forward, maintaining the spine straight and the neck in a neutral position.

Things To Be Cared For:

- Do not practice this pose if you are suffering from asthma, diarrhea, a lower back injury, or lumbar disc herniation.
- People with neck, shoulder, lower back, or knee pain should avoid this pose or practice under the supervision of a therapeutic yoga teacher.
- Women who are pregnant or are in their menstrual cycle should avoid this asana.

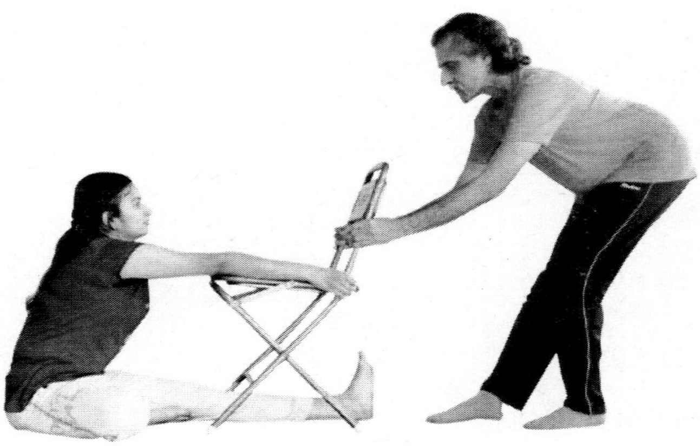

Urdhva Mukha Janu Sirsasana
Variation 1

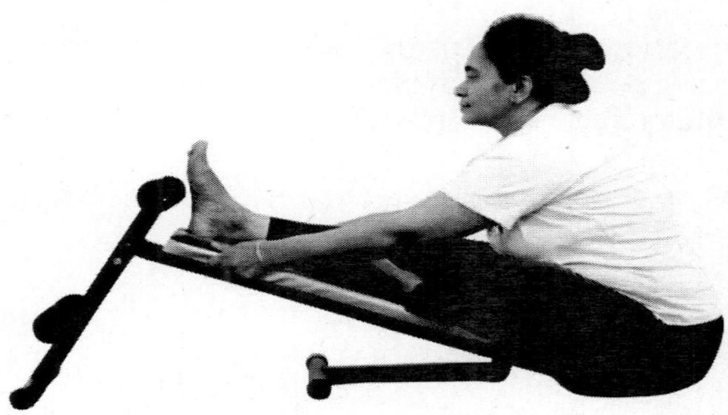

Urdhva Mukha Janu Sirsasana
Variation 2

9. Marichyasana I (Sage Marichi's Pose):

Steps To Perform:

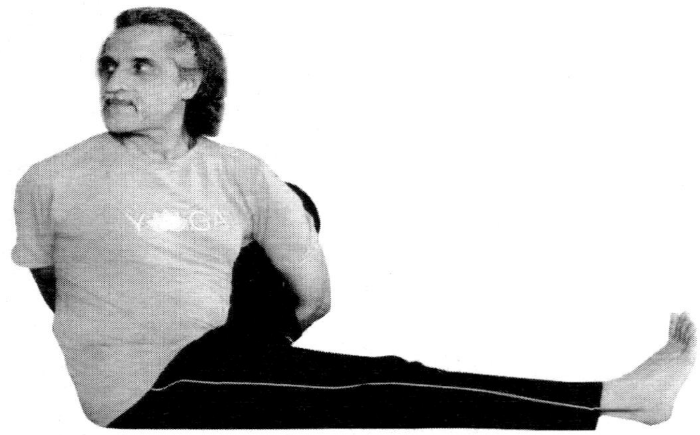

1. Sit in Dandasana.
2. Bend the left knee, with the kneecap pointing towards the ceiling.
3. Lean forward, bring the left armpit close to the inner edges of the left knee, fold the left arm in front of the shin, taking it behind, and clasp the right hand behind the back.
4. Inhale, lift the spine, exhale, and twist the torso to the right.
5. Stay and breathe here for 30 seconds to 1 minute.
6. Exhale, come back to Dandasana, and repeat on the other side.

Joint Actions:

- Lateral rotation of the spine.
- Extension of shoulders and slight abduction.
- Flexion of elbows with forearm pronation and wrist neutral.
- Hip flexion with adduction of the bent leg.
- Hip in neutral and extension of knee in the extended leg.

Main Muscle Actions:

- Lateral rotators of the lumbar and cervical muscles.
- Flexor group of hip and knee muscles.
- Shoulder extensors and adductor muscle groups.

Things To Focus On:

- Focus on engaging the buttock and heel on the extended leg and the sole of the foot of the bent leg to create a stable base.
- Engage the hip flexors and thighs of the outstretched leg and maintain the leg straight.

- While twisting, engage the shoulders by drawing the shoulder blades together and keeping the chest open.
- Keep the neck neutral and the shoulders in line with each other.

Things To Be Cared For:

- People who have diarrhea should avoid this asana.
- People suffering from asthma, hip, neck, knee, shoulder, back, or spine injuries and with recent abdominal, brain, or heart surgeries should practice this asana under the supervision of a therapeutic yoga teacher.

Marichyasana I Variation 1

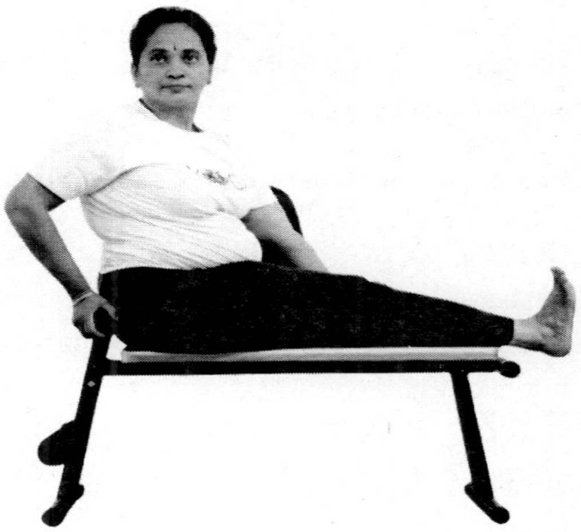

Marichyasana I Variation 1 Other Side

Marichyasana I Variation 2

Treatment:

Ayurveda:

Ayurvedic treatment is based on the type of dosha imbalance. However, some of the common treatment options, according to age and condition, may include:

- Langhana
- Swedana
- Deepana
- Shodhana
- Virechana (therapeutic purgation) helps to restore the absorption process and remove excess water from the body.
- Vasti (medicated enemas): cleansing of the colon, which houses Vata energy.
- Eraṇḍa patra pinda swedana. Some of the herbs used in arthritis are ashwagandha, dashmoola, trikatu churna, boswellia serrata, and guggulu. Some oils used in treatment are bala, bala ashwagandha, maha narayana thailam, and pinda thailam.

Allopathy:

- NSAIDs
- Disease-modifying antirheumatic drugs (DMARDs)
- Immunosuppressants
- Topical steroids
- Biologic agents
- Steroid injections:
- Joint replacement surgery

Pranayama:

- Abdominal breathing.
- Viloma Pranayama (3 levels).
- Bhastrika.
- Surya Bheda Pranayama.
- Nadi Shodhana.

Nutrition for Arthritis:

Arthritis is caused by various factors, some of which are inflammation in the joints, weakness, and obesity. When it comes to food, there is no specific diet for arthritis, but a diet rich in whole foods like fruits, vegetables, nuts, grains, anti-inflammatory foods, foods rich in calcium, and other vitamins and minerals is not only great for overall health but also helps manage the disease actively.

Foods to Consume:

Anti-Inflammatory Foods	Fresh fruits and vegetables, green leafy vegetables
Calcium Rich Foods	Milk and milk products, soybeans, spinach etc.
Omega 3 Fatty Acids	Fish like sardines, mackerel, salmon
Nuts & Seeds	Flax seeds, chia seeds, walnuts, almonds, peanuts, cashews, pistachios, sunflower seeds
Whole Grains	Oats, ragi, wheat, brown rice, quinoa, barley
Plant Protein	Soya chunks, soybeans, tofu, chickpeas, lentils
Animal Protein	Eggs, chicken, turkey
Others	Water - drink plenty of water to keep yourself hydrated, improve fluid content in the body and maintain body temperature. Ghee - contains vitamin K and helps in absorption of calcium. It's beneficial to improve bone strength.

Foods to Avoid:

- Saturated fats: butter, cheese, palm oil, coconut oil, etc.
- Oily, fried, and fatty foods.

- High sodium intake: packaged food and processed food.
- Sugary foods like sweets, chocolates, cereals, etc.
- Smoking and alcohol.

It's important to follow a well-balanced diet to get all the vitamins and minerals that your body needs. A variety of fresh fruits, vegetables, nuts, whole grains, protein, and dairy are required to fuel your body with proper nutrition. This will help to keep weight under control and will also help to cut down on excess weight. The practice of yoga can be beneficial for managing arthritis.

VARICOSE VEINS

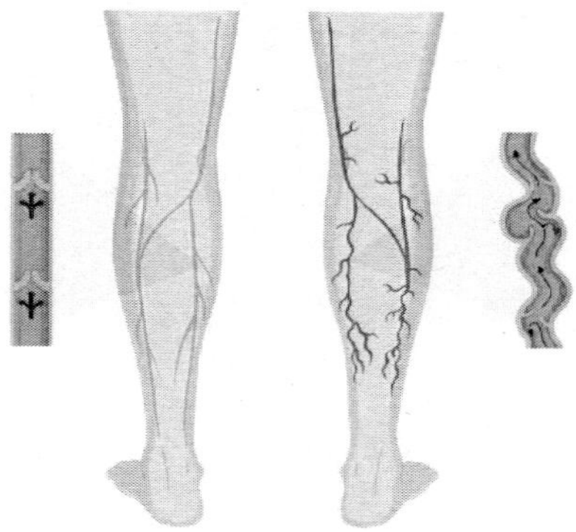

VARICOSE VEIN

Varicose veins are larger and twisted veins that are visible mainly beneath the surface of the skin. These veins are swollen and can be seen in dark purple, blue, or red. Any vein in the body may develop into varicose. Mainly, the veins in the legs, feet, and back of the calves are affected. Prolonged standing increases the pressure in the veins, resulting in varicose veins.

Varicose veins develop because those veins, which carry blood towards the heart, stop functioning efficiently. When the valves of the veins become weak or damaged, they cannot carry blood against the force of gravity, resulting in the accumulation of blood in the veins, which appears swollen and enlarged.

Some types of varicose veins include:

1. **Saphenous Varicose Veins:** These are predominantly in the saphenous veins (the longest vein) in the legs, which swell larger and bulge out from the skin, and the veins appear very big. They can be colorless but visible as they protrude out.

2. **Reticular Varicose Veins:** These veins spread across the skin like a mesh. They are generally thick and appear in red, green, or purple. Although they do not bulge, they can be very ugly to look at.

3. **Spider Veins:** These are small, red, or blue in color and can be anywhere on the body. Spider veins usually spread in a web shape and are also thinner and smaller compared to other varicose veins. They do not make the skin bulge out like varicose veins.

According to Ayurveda, varicose veins can be determined as Siraja Granthi. "Sirija" means "veins," and "granthi" means "knot" or "cyst-like swelling." Varicose veins are predominantly a Vata disorder affecting the Rakta Dhatu; however, they can be caused by an imbalance in any of the three doshas. It is predominantly caused by an imbalance in Vyana Vata and Agni at the level of Dhatu, creating increased pressure and affecting the valves and elasticity of the veins. Vata by itself or along with Kapha gets vitiated in weight-bearing areas like thighs, calves, and ankles, and these imbalanced doshas obstruct the flow of blood, causing varicose veins.

Ayurveda classified varicose veins into the following types:

- Vataja
- Pittaja
- Kaphaja
- Medhaja
- Siraja

Causes:

Some of the common causes of varicose veins include:

- Prolonged standing or sitting.
- Obesity.
- Sedentary lifestyle.
- Genetics.
- Aging.
- Consumption of birth control pills.
- Pregnancy or menopause.
- Chronic constipation causes hemorrhoids.
- Injury.

Symptoms:

The main symptoms of varicose veins are varied in visibility. Each one may experience symptoms differently; however, the most common symptoms of varicose veins include:

- Veins look swollen, twisted, or bulged.
- Throbbing pain, numbness, burning, and muscle cramps in the veins.
- Discoloration of the skin.
- Heaviness in the legs, especially at night.
- Itching and rashes.
- Inflammation of the skin and hardening of the veins.

- An injury to the affected vein can lead to heavy bleeding.
- Clots can be seen in the veins.

Diagnosis:

- Medical history.
- Physical exam.
- Duplex ultrasound.

Yogic Intervention:

Various studies have shown that a combination of inverted poses and other asanas that invigorate the muscular movements involving the calf muscles are helpful for varicose veins. Performing an inverted pose, where the legs are lifted and the feet are resting up against the wall, allows gravity to do the important work of returning blood and removing blocks in the veins. Regular practice of asanas improves circulation and tones the muscles, thereby reducing the risk of developing varicose veins or worsening the existing condition. Also, making a few lifestyle changes and following a proper diet to keep weight under control is extremely beneficial for people suffering from varicose veins.

Case Study:

Subjective: Mr. Shekar (name changed) a 35-year-old employee in a private firm, had come with problems in his legs. He said he had to spend long periods of time standing at work.

Objective: Shekar was advised to consult a neurologist for his condition.

Assessment: After investigations done by the neurologist, he was diagnosed with varicose veins, which caused the pain.

Plan: Shekar was advised to take medication, use stockings, and take up yoga classes for relief.

Shekar took up the yoga therapy sessions and found good relief after 10 sessions. Now, Shekar is a regular yoga practitioner, hardly uses the stockings, and has no signs of varicose veins in his legs.

- **Surya Namaskar (Sun Salutations):**

Regular practice of Surya Namaskars can be beneficial.

- **Asanas (Yoga Postures):**

The following are some postures that are helpful in managing varicose veins:

1. Nrityasana (Dancer's Pose):

Steps To Perform:

1. Stand in Tadasana with the feet hip-width apart.
2. Exhale, turn the feet outwards, and sink the hips.
3. Raise the heels up and come up on the toes.
4. Extend both arms above the head and hold the palms in Chin Mudra.
5. Stay and breathe here for 30 seconds to 1 minute.
6. Come back to Tadasana.

Joint Actions:

- Spin in a neutral position.
- Flexion of the shoulder with extension of elbows with a mid-prone position of the forearm.
- Hip abduction, internal rotation with knee flexion, and ankle plantar flexion.

Main Muscle Actions:

- Contraction of the hip flexors and abductor muscle groups.
- Contraction of hamstring and gastrocnemius, soleus muscles.
- It stretches the levator scapulae.

Things To Focus On:

- Engage the toes by spreading them wide; focus on engaging the feet by inverting the feet slightly and raising the heels.
- Engage the hip flexors, abductors, and thighs to sink, and abduct the hips to feel a stretch around the groin.
- Engage the core by drawing the navel in, tucking the tailbone back, and engaging the spinal extensors and flexors to maintain a neutral spine.

Things To Be Cared For:

- People suffering from injuries to the ankle, knee, or hip should avoid practicing this pose.

Nrityasana Variation 1

2. Natarajasana (Lord Of The Dance Pose):

"Nataraja" is one of the names given to Lord Shiva in his form as the cosmic dancer.

Steps To Perform:

1. Stand in Tadasana, bend the right knee, and grasp the right ankle with the right hand.
2. Inhale, lift the spine, exhale, stretch the right leg back, move the heel away from the buttock, and bring the chest forward. Extend the left arm forward, holding the fingers in the chin mudra, gaze at the fingertips, and gently arch the back to open the chest.
3. Stay and breathe here for 30 seconds to 1 minute.
4. Exhale, come out of the pose, and repeat on the other side.

Joint Actions:

- Extension of the spine.
- Extension of the knee of the standing leg.
- Slight extension of the hip, knee flexion, and plantar flexion of the ankle of the lifted leg.
- Flexion of the shoulder and extension of the elbow of the forward hand.
- Extension of the shoulder, extension of the elbow, and forearm pronation of the backside arm.

Main Muscle Actions:

- Contraction of the erector spinae, gluteus minimus, and hamstring muscles.
- Stretching of the hip flexor group of muscles of the elevated leg.

Things To Focus On:

- Engage the core by drawing the navel in, squeezing the glutes, and tucking the tailbone.
- Engage the hip extensors, the back of the thighs, and the toes; bend the knee; and stretch the leg up.
- Engage the hip flexors, thighs, and the foot on the standing leg to maintain a stable base.
- Engage the spinal extensors and begin to arch the back, maintaining the length of the spine.
- Engage the flexors of the hand and fingers to rotate the forearm and grasp the foot. (Modified Pose 1—with rope)

Things To Be Cared For:

- People suffering from high blood pressure, hernia, colitis, a weak heart, a duodenal ulcer, vertigo, carpal tunnel syndrome, or a slip disc should avoid practicing this pose.
- During pregnancy, women should practice this pose under the supervision of a therapeutic yoga teacher.

Natrajasana Variation 1

Natrajasana Variation 2

3. Garudasana (Eagle Pose):

Steps To Perform:

1. Stand in Tadasana.
2. Bend the knees, lift the left leg, cross it over the right leg, bring the left thigh over the right thigh, and lock the legs.
3. Bring the arms forward and cross the right arm over the left arm.
4. Turn the hands with the palms facing each other, press the palms together, and gaze forward.
5. Stay and breathe here for 30 seconds to 1 minute.
6. Inhale, come out of the pose, and repeat on the other side.

Joint Actions:

- Mild flexion of the hip with flexion of the knees.
- Neutral position of the spine.
- Adduction of the shoulder with mild flexion.
- Flexion of the elbows with pronation of the forearm.

Main Muscle Actions:

- Contraction of the hip and knee flexor groups of muscles on the bent leg.
- Contraction of the gluteus and quadriceps muscles on the extended leg.
- Contraction of the shoulder and elbow flexor muscle groups.

Things To Focus On:

- Engage the shoulder blades by moving them away from each other, and interlock the hands while engaging the upper arms.
- Engage the thighs by contracting them, and engage the hip flexors to interlock the legs. Focus on pointing the toes of the overlapped foot downward.
- Engage the core by drawing the navel in and tucking the tailbone back, and keep lengthening the spine to avoid rounding the back.

Things To Be Cared For:

- People with elbow, knee, shoulder, and ankle injuries should avoid practicing this pose.
- People suffering from varicose veins behind their knees should avoid practicing this pose.
- Women should avoid practicing this pose during pregnancy.

Garudasana Variation 1

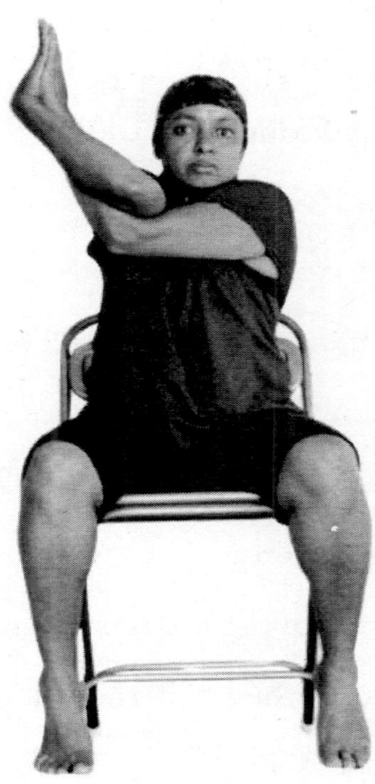

Garudasana Variation 2

4. Virasana (Hero Pose):

Steps To Perform:

1. Sit in Vajrasana with your knees together.
2. Slide the feet away by the side of the buttocks and sit in between the heels.
3. Hands extended in front of the knees in Chin Mudra.
4. Maintain the back straight.
5. Stay here and breathe for 30 seconds to 1 minute.
6. Release and come back to Vajrasana.

Joint Actions:

- Neutral position of the spine.
- Mild shoulder flexion with elbow extension.
- Hip flexion, adduction, and internal rotation.
- Knee flexion with ankle plantar flexion.

Main Muscle Actions:

- Contraction of the hip flexors and knee flexors muscle groups.
- Stretching of the tibialis anterior muscles.

Things To Focus On:

- Focus on internally rotating the hips, joining the knees together, and bringing the buttocks in between the heels.
- Engage the core by drawing the navel in, pushing the tailbone back, and maintaining the length in the spine.

- Keep the chin parallel to the floor and the neck relaxed.

Things To Be Cared For:

- People with chronic headaches and heart problems should avoid performing this pose.
- People with injuries to the knee or ankle should practice this pose under the supervision of a therapeutic yoga teacher.

Veerasana Variation 1

Veerasana Variation 2

5. **Kapotasana (Pigeon Pose):**

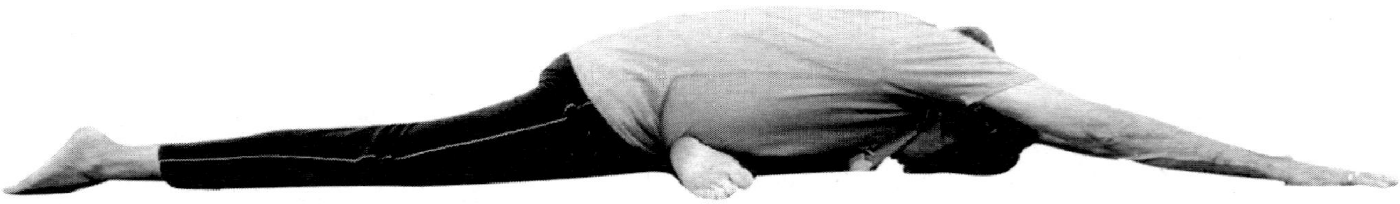

Steps To Perform:

1. Begin with Adho Mukha Shvanasana.
2. Inhale, bring the left knee forward, place it close to the left wrist, and place the foot close to the right wrist.
3. Bring the pelvis down towards the floor and stretch the right leg back, dropping the right knee down, toes pointing back.
4. Exhale, fold forward, extend the arms, and bring the forehead down.
5. Stay and breathe here for 30 seconds to 1 minute.
6. Inhale, lift the head and chest, exhale, come back to Adho Mukha Shvanasana, and repeat on the other side.

Joint Actions:

- Hip flexion and knee flexion of the front leg.
- Extension of the hip with extension of the knee of the back leg.
- Neutral position of the spine.
- Slight abduction of the shoulder with elbow flexion and forearm pronation.

Main Muscle Actions:

- Contraction of the hip and knee flexor groups of muscles on the bent knee.
- Stretching of the hip flexor muscles of the extended leg.
- Contraction of the rectus and transversus abdominis muscles.

Things To Focus On:

- Engage the hip flexors and extensors, then stretch the legs. Focus on engaging the thighs and toes to get the pelvis as close as possible to the floor, and try to keep the hips in line.
- Engage the core by drawing the navel in and tucking the tailbone back. Engage the spinal extensors to extend the spine.

- Engage the shoulders and the hands in the stretch.

Things To Be Cared For:

- People with spine, hip, shoulder, and knee injuries or people suffering from insomnia, migraine, hypertension, spondylitis, and weak functions of any organ should avoid practicing this pose.
- Women should avoid practicing this pose during pregnancy and menstrual cycles.

Kapotasana Variation 1

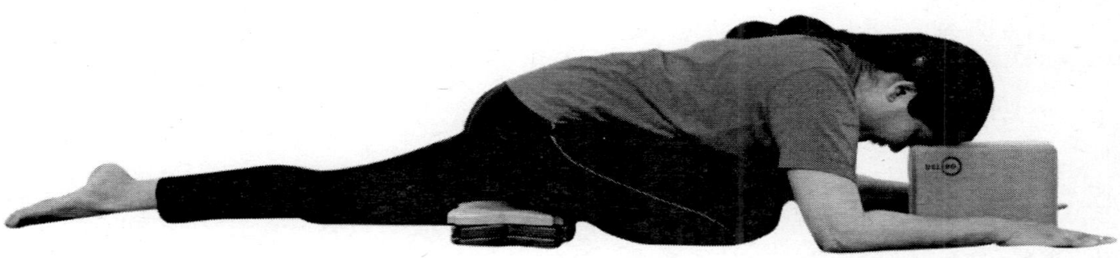

Kapotasana Variation 2

6. Anantasana (Sleeping Vishnu Pose):

Steps To Perform:

1. Lie down on the back, turn laterally to the left side, keep the legs outstretched, bend the left elbow, and rest the head on the palm.
2. Inhale, bend the right knee, and grab hold of the big toe with the index, middle finger, and thumb.
3. Exhale and straighten the right leg up towards the ceiling.
4. Stay and breathe here for 30 seconds to 1 minute.
5. Exhale, release, and repeat on the other side.

Joint Actions:

- Flexion and abduction of the hip of the elevated leg, extension of the knee, and neutral position of the ankle.
- Lateral flexion of the spine.
- Abduction of the shoulder with extension of the elbow on the top arm.
- Abduction of the shoulder with flexion of the elbow of the bottom arm.
- Lateral flexion of the cervical spine.

Main Muscle Actions:

- Contraction of the quadratus lumborum, hip abductor muscles, and knee extensor muscle group of the elevated leg.
- Stretching of the hamstring and gastrocnemius muscles of the elevated leg..

Things To Focus On:

- Engage the spinal extensors and internal and external obliques to turn the body sideways.
- Engage the quadriceps to flex the hip and extend the knee.
- There should be no pressure on the neck.
- Engage the hamstrings and the heel of the foot to stretch the leg upwards.

Things To Be Cared For:

- People suffering from high or low blood pressure, neck or shoulder injuries, or back pain should avoid practicing the pose.

Ananthasana Variation 1

Ananthasana Variation 2

7. Ananda Balasana (Happy Baby Pose):

Steps To Perform:

1. Lie on your back.
2. Bend the knees, bring them close to the chest, and widen the knees.
3. Bring the elbows close to the inner edges of the knees, grab hold of the outer edges of the soles of the feet, point them towards the ceiling, and separate the feet.
4. Inhale, and while exhaling, pull the feet down towards the floor, bringing the knees closer to the armpits, and widen the legs to deepen the stretch.
5. Stay and breathe here for 30 seconds to 1 minute.
6. Release and come back to the laying-down position.

Joint Actions:

- Neutral position of the spine.
- Flexion of hips, flexion of knees, and ankle dorsiflexion.
- Slight flexion and abduction of the shoulders.
- Flexion of the elbows with a mid-prone position of the forearm.

Main Muscle Actions:

- Contraction of the hip flexors and knee flexor group of muscles.
- Stretching of gluteal muscles.

Things To Focus On:

- Engage the core by pressing the tailbone and the sacrum down to the floor, and keep lifting the heels up while pulling back with the arms.
- Engage the shoulders and the neck by pressing both the back of the neck and the shoulders down to the floor.

Things To Be Cared For:

- People with hip, knee, or shoulder injuries should avoid practicing this pose.
- Women during pregnancy and menstrual cycles should avoid practicing this pose.

Ananda Balasana Variation 1

Ananda Balasana Variation 2

8. Urdhva Prasarita Padasana (Upward Extended Feet Pose):

Steps To Perform:

1. Lie on the back with the legs stretched forward and arms by the side of the body.
2. Inhale and lift the legs up gradually to 60 and 90 degrees.
3. Stay at each angle for 15 to 30 seconds.
4. Exhale and gently bring both legs down.

Joint Actions:

- Flexion of the shoulder, extension of the elbow, and supination of the forearm.
- Flexion and adduction of the hip with knee extension and ankle in a neutral position.

Main Muscle Actions:

- Contraction of the rectus, transversus abdominis, and hip flexor muscle groups.
- Stretching of the lumbosacral, hamstring, and gastrocnemius muscles.

Things To Focus On:

- Engage the core by drawing the navel in, engaging the legs, and pressing the thighs against each other. Focus on pushing the heels towards the ceiling.
- Keep the chest, spine, and neck relaxed.

Things To Be Cared For:

- People with recent abdominal, hip, or sciatica surgeries should avoid practicing this pose.
- People suffering from injuries to the neck or lower back pain should practice this under the supervision of a therapeutic yoga teacher.

➢ Women should avoid practicing this pose during pregnancy and the menstrual cycle.

Urdhva Prasarita Paddotanasana
Variation 60 1

Urdhva Prasarita Paddotanasana
Variation 60 2

Urdhva Prasarita Paddotanasana
Variation 90 1

Urdhva Prasarita Paddotanasana
Variation 90 2

Urdhva Prasarita Paddotanasana
Variation 90 3

9. Urdva Pada Kriya (Supine Scissor Kicks):

Steps To Perform:

1. Lie down on the back with the legs stretched forward and the hands by the side of the buttocks.
2. Lift the legs up 90 degrees.
3. Slightly bend the knees and start shaking the legs gently for about 20 to 30 times.
4. Come back to a neutral position.

Joint Actions:

- Neutral position of the shoulder with elbow extension and forearm pronation.
- Neutral position of the spine.
- Flexion and adduction of the hip with extension of the knees.

Main Muscle Actions:

- Contraction of the rectus and transversus abdominis muscles.
- Contraction of hip flexors and knee flexor group muscles.
- Stretching of gluteal muscles.

Things To Focus On:

- Engage the core by drawing the navel in, engage the legs by pressing the thighs against each other, and point the toes towards the ceiling.
- Keep the chest, spine, and neck relaxed.

Things To Be Cared For:

- People with recent abdominal, hip, or sciatica surgeries should avoid practicing this pose.
- People suffering from injuries to the neck or lower back pain should practice this under the supervision of a therapeutic yoga teacher.
- Women should avoid practicing this pose during pregnancy and the menstrual cycle.

Urdhva Pada Kriya 1

Urdhva Pada Kriya 2

Treatment:

Ayurveda:

Ayurvedic treatment varies based on the dominance of the dosha. However, some ayurvedic treatments could include:

- Abhyanga (gentle massage or application of oil).
- Swedana (Sauna).
- Yapnana Basti.
- Avagahana Krama (dipping the leg in Eranda Taila and Dashmoola Kwatha).
- Siravyadha (bloodletting therapy).
- Jalauka Charan (leech therapy).

Allopathy:

- Compression stockings.
- Thermal ablation.
- Elevation of the legs.
- Sclerotherapy.
- Micro phlebectomy.
- Vein stripping.

Pranayama:

- Abdominal breathing.
- Viloma pranayama (3 levels).
- Ujjayi pranayama.
- Nadi shodhana.

Nutrition for Varicose Veins:

Varicose veins can be caused by hormonal changes in estrogen and progesterone. In women, this problem is more prevalent than in men. These hormones play a role in menstrual cycles and childbirth. Varicose veins, especially in the legs, can result from monthly hormonal fluctuations in women. As women approach menopause, these fluctuations become more significant. Increased production of estrogen and progesterone can weaken veins and affect their valves, which control blood flow. Varicose veins are not exclusive to women; as men age, lower testosterone levels make estrogen and progesterone more dominant, contributing to varicose veins.

However, lifestyle changes can reverse this condition. While there is no specific diet for treating varicose veins, adopting a healthy diet and regular exercise can enhance blood circulation throughout the body, promoting overall health.

Foods to Consume:

Vegetables	Green leafy vegetables, beetroots, broccoli, carrots
Whole Grain	Wheat, barley, oats, ragi, quinoa
Seeds	Flax seeds and chia seeds
Food Rich in Vitamin C	Citrus fruits like oranges, kiwi, pineapples, tomatoes, strawberries, bell peppers are a great source of vitamin C
Food Rich in Vitamin E	Sunflower seeds, avocados, dark leafy vegetables, papaya, mango are a great source of vitamin E, which acts as a natural blood thinner and helps prevent clots
Foods Rich in Antioxidants	Apples, bananas, berries, grapes, onions, prunes, apples, raisins help release toxins from the body
Others	Fiber keeps you fuller for longer, its integral for digestion and helps maintain a healthy weight. Vitamin C is essential to keep your veins healthy. It provides your veins with collagen and elasticity. Ginger - increases blood circulation and breaks down fibrin in the blood vessels which prevent the veins from hardening. Water - drink enough water to keep yourself hydrated, balance the temperature of the body, helps your body keep a healthy balance of fluids.

Foods to Avoid:

- **Salty:** Excessive sodium can lead to water retention, increasing blood pressure, and putting strain on the venous system.
- **High-sugar foods:** Avoid items like cereals, sweets, and chocolates.
- **Saturated fat:** Limit the intake of butter, palm oil, and coconut oil.
- **Calorie-dense food:** Be cautious with high-calorie foods.
- **Constipation-inducing food:** Minimize the consumption of highly processed food, red meat, fried items, and excessive dairy products.
- **Alcohol:** It can cause dehydration and sluggishness in the veins.

Adopting a well-balanced diet, incorporating regular exercise, and maintaining consistency in these changes will contribute to weight management and alleviate varicose vein issues.

SOURCES & REFERENCES

STRESS

https://www.verywellmind.com/

https://www.mentalhealth.org.uk/

https://www.healthline.com/

Sushruta Samhita edited by Jadavji Trikamji

Charaka Samhita edited by P V Sharma Vol. I & I

CERVICAL

https://www.mayoclinic.org/

https://www.spine-health.com/

https://www.spineuniverse.com/

https://umiamihealth.org/

https://www.columbianeurology.org/

https://www.emoryhealthcare.org/

https://mayfieldclinic.com/

https://orthoinfo.aaos.org/

https://www.umms.org/

https://www.sciencedirect.com/

Chaturvedi G ChikitsaSthana, Charaka Samhita of Agnivesha

Chaturvedi G Sutra Sthana, Charaka Samhita of Agnivesha

Bhavaprakasha Nighantu Indian Materia Medica of Shri. Bhavamishra

BhaisajyaRatnavali of Govinda Das Ji Bhisagratna

THYROID

https://www.webmd.com

https://www.medicinenet.com/

https://my.clevelandclinic.org/

https://www.healthline.com/

Effective Ayurveda therapy to treat thyroid disorders by AnumodKakkassery A, Krishnan P, Varghese PR.

Chakrapani Datta, Commentator. Charaka Samhita of Agnivesha, edited by Yadavji T., ChikitsaSthaana. Ch.15

S.KamalakarPuripanda, Renuka.M, S M.Vaidya. The Role of SiraaVyadhana in Treating BhasmakRoga (Atyagni). International Journal of Ayurveda and Pharma Research 2016

Nutrition ref: https://www.tandfonline.com/doi/abs/10.3109/09637486.2012.704904

ASTHMA

https://www.mayoclinic.org/

https://www.healthline.com/

Acharya Agnivesha Charaka Samhita edited by Vaidya Yadavji Trikamji

Sushruta Samhita edited by Vaidya Yadavji Trikamji

HYPERTENSION

https://www.who.int/

https://www.healthline.com/

https://www.mayoclinic.org/

https://my.clevelandclinic.org/

https://www.webmd.com/

https://www.healio.com/

https://www.heart.org/

Sushruta Samhita edited by Jadavji Trikamji

Charaka Samhita edited by P V Sharma Vol. I & II

ACIDITY AND GASTRITIS

https://www.webmd.com/

https://www.healthline.com/

https://www.mayoclinic.org/

https://my.clevelandclinic.org/

AgniveshaCharaka Samhita, Shri Satyanarayan Shastri elaborated Vidyotinihindi commentary by Pt. Kashinath Shastri and Gorakhnath Chaturvedi, ChikitsaSthana 15/44 – 47; 460, 1/60 page 36. Chapter 15, Vimana Sthana 2/9, Sutra Sthana 25/40

Sushruta Samhita edited by KavirajaAbhika Dutta Shastri, Sutra Sthana 2/11 page 116, Uttara Tantra

DIABETES

https://medlineplus.gov/diabetes.html

https://www.medicinenet.com/

https://www.healthline.com/

https://www.diabetes.co.uk/yoga-and-diabetes.html#

Charaka Samhita Chikitsa Sthana by Agnivesha

Sushruta Samhita by Kaviraj Kunjlal Bhishagranta

Ashtanga Hridhyam Chikitasa Sthana, Vagbhata Nidana Sthana

A practical handbook of Panchakarma Procedures CCRAS 2009

Nutrition Ref: https://pubmed.ncbi.nlm.nih.gov/28606215/

https://www.ncbi.nlm.nih.gov/pmc/articles/PMC4876745/

https://www.ncbi.nlm.nih.gov/pmc/articles/PMC2424054/

LUMBAR ISSUES

https://www.spine-health.com/

https://www.webmd.com/

https://www.spineuniverse.com

Charaka Samhita Chikitsa Sthana

Charaka Samhita Sutra Sthana

Charaka Samhita Siddhi Sthana

ARTHRITIS

https://www.verywellmind.com/

https://www.mentalhealth.org.uk/

https://www.healthline.com/

https://www.hopkinsarthritis.org/

https://www.medicinenet.com/

https://www.arthritis.org/

https://www.mayoclinic.org/

Madhava Kara, Madhava Nidana, with Madhukosh Sanskrit commentary by Sri Vijaya Rakshita and Srikantha Datta

The Vidyotini Hindi Commentary by Sri Sudarsana Sastri - edited by Prof. Yadunandan Upadhayaya, Ravindra Tripathi

Charaka Samhita - Vidya Manorama Hindi commentary

VARICOSE VEINS

https://www.stylecraze.com/

https://www.varikostop.in/

https://msdmanuals.com/

https://www.andiappanyoga.com/

https://www.asanajournal.com/

https://www.easyayurveda.com/

Shalya Tantra Vignanam Dr. M. Rama Sundara Rao

Ross and Wilson, Anatomy and Physiology

Astanga Hrdayam Vidyotini Hindi Commentary written by Kaviraj Atrideva Gupta

Caraka Samhita Vidyotini Hindi Translation by Kashinath Pandey 'Sastri'

Ayurveda: A fruitful remedy for varicose veins, Jaipur National institute of Ayurveda March 2016

Dr P.V. Sharma - Dravyaguna Vijnna Vol-2

BOOKS REFERRED

- Light On Yoga - B.K.S. Iyengar
- Path To Holistic Health - B.K.S. Iyengar
- Asana Pranayama Mudra & Bandha - Swami Satyananda Saraswati (Bihar Yoga School)
- Experiment & Experience On The Chair - H.S. Arun
- Moving Toward Balance - Rodney Yee
- Light On Pranayama - B.K.S. Iyengar
- Hatha Yoga Pradipika - Swami Mukti Bodhananda
- Prana, Pranayama, Prana Vidya - Niranjanananda Saraswati
- Yoga & Your Health - Dr M.L. Gharote
- Hearth Of Yoga - T. Desikachar
- Human Anatomy - B.D. Chaurasia
- Yoga Anatomy by - Leslie Kaminoff and Amy Mathews

IMAGES

1. Lumbar issues.jpeg:

https://www.physio-pedia.com/Lumbar_Spondylosis

2. Acidity&Gastritis.jpg:

https://www.freepik.com/free-vector/gastroesophageal-reflux-disease-anatomy_2840999.htm

3. Stress.jpg:

https://www.freepik.com/free-vector/flat-design-schizophrenia-illustration_24997085.htm

4. Thyroid.jpg:

https://www.freepik.com/free-vector/hand-drawn-flat-design-thyroid-illustration_23177000.htm

5. Diabetes.jpg

:https://www.freepik.com/free-vector/realistic-pancreas-anatomy-medical-composition-with-editable-text-captions-pointing-colored-parts-internal-organs-vector-illustration_28795248.htm

6. Arthritis.jpg:

https://www.freepik.com/free-vector/diagram-showing-rheumatoid-arthritis-hand_1046928.htm

7. Varicose Veins.jpg:

https://www.freepik.com/free-vector/human-legs-with-varicose-vein_28768312.htm

8. Excavation during the Indus Valley Civilization.png:

https://wellcomecollection.org/series/WjATLCsAAC4Ae-PS

9. Ayurveda(2).jpg:

https://www.slideshare.net/ANANDKATTI2/dr-anand-katti-52792830

10. Ayurveda (1).jpg:

https://www.freepik.com/free-photo/front-view-cinnamon-mint-alogn-with-fresh-tea-white-ingredients-spices-color_9909574.htm

11. Food and Nutrition.jpg:

https://www.freepik.com/free-photo/top-view-medicinal-spices-herbs_11375791.htm

12. Goal of Yoga.jpg:

https://www.freepik.com/free-ai-image/serene-silhouette-meditating-tranquil-autumn-mountain-generated-by-ai_41366727.htm

Shri Upanishath Yoga Center Trust Regd.
804, 1st cross, E and F block, Manujapatha Road, Kuvempunagar, Mysuru
570023
Phone: 7026000633 Email: yogasudhesh@gmail.com
Youtube: Shri Upanishath Yoga Center
Facebook: Shri Upanishath Yoga Center Trust Regd.
Instagram: shri.upanishath.yoga.centre